AN ENGLISHMAN'S COOKERY JOURNEY

FROM ALDEBURGH TO AIX-EN-PROVENCE

RICHARD FREEMAN

Illustrated by Tessa Newcomb

also featuring drawings by Jason Gathorne-Hardy and a watercolour by Karen Freeman

Foreword by Lady Cranbrook

For DK

An Englishman's Cookery Journey

First published by Flatford Press, Court Street, Nayland, Suffolk CO6 4JL

Paintings © Tessa Newcomb
Line drawings © Jason Gathorne-Hardy
Watercolour © Karen Freeman

British Library Cataloguing-In-Publication Data.
A catalogue record for this book is available from the British Library.

ISBN 978-1-5272-4620-1

Printed and bound in Suffolk by The Lavenham Press Ltd

Design by Alexander Ford
Design consultant Deborah Mack
Dustjacket illustration by Tessa Newcomb

Typeset in 11 point Monotype Bembo

Flatford Press is committed to a sustainable future for its business, its readers and the planet. This book is made from and printed on FSC papers.

CONTENTS

On some September evenings everything seems to fall in place

FOREWORD

East Anglia has for centuries been the larder for London, with a reputation that extends back to the Middle Ages and even earlier. Its livestock and poultry, together with its agricultural and horticultural produce, have always been known for their excellence. Only more recently has this reputation extended to include local food.

One of Suffolk's greatest assets is the huge variety, quality and abundance of our locally produced food and drink, available in our high street and village shops, farmer's markets, on our beaches from our fishermen, in our hotels, pubs and bed-and-breakfasts – and of course at our food festivals. There are so many opportunities to buy fresh, seasonal, locally distinctive food. And by doing this we can obtain the ingredients for delicious meals and at the same time we can improve our diet. Another advantage to buying local is that it helps to preserve our precious food heritage and provides an economic seedbed for innovation, supporting the whole local economy. Buying local food is what keeps our countryside alive, supporting our market towns and villages and our local fishing industry. Searching for local food is highly rewarding – and above all it is very enjoyable. Richard Freeman will help you do this. His book provides an interesting and informative introduction to the pleasures of buying Suffolk food. It is a guide not only to the amazing variety of local food and drink which can be found, but it also includes excellent recipes. Some are traditional, some his own. They are easy to follow and, like all good cookery books, a delight to read. The book will live on the kitchen shelf, but I am sure, also like all the best cookery books, it will be read by many just for the pleasure of learning about Suffolk and its food.

Caroline Cranbrook

Lady Cranbrook OBE
Great Glemham
Suffolk
2019

Indian Runners

PROLOGUE

This imaginary journey, from Aldeburgh on the bracing Suffolk coast to the sunshine of Aix-en-Provence in the South of France, is the story of how I taught myself to cook – a journey which has brought me a better understanding of a vast and fascinating subject.

It tells of what I cook, what I love, what I buy and what I do to enable me to produce something interesting, appetising and healthy for my table at home. That story goes on every day and every month of every year in my own kitchen and it has been written for anyone who feels they might like to follow in my footsteps, with this book as a loyal companion by their side.

I have had the privilege of living in this lovely county of Suffolk for 40 years. It is a tranquil place, where locals go and strangers come, where we, whose county it is, do our work in our own, unhurried, quiet way. Although less than one hundred miles from metropolitan pandemonium, Suffolk carefully takes account of the seasons as they pass, seasons unnoticed or often unknown to those pursuing the inexorable progress of globalisation at the other end of the railway line. Here in Suffolk the seasons are all important. The production of livestock, the growing of fruit and vegetables and the practice of sustainable fishing coupled with responsible, modern husbandry has made the county into a much valued food destination.

I am fortunate enough to have had another privilege too. That is to have worked in France and with the French, as well as being able to visit that lovely country almost every year of my life from an early age. For as long as I can remember I have admired French cuisine, but it is to the cuisine of Provence that I am particularly attracted and which I celebrate in this book. The favourable climate, the olives, the olive oils, the herbs, the fish, the garlic, the tomatoes, the vegetables, the fruit, the cheeses as well as the wines form the many cornerstones of a wonderfully colourful and healthy cuisine.

Anyone who wants to set out on the cookery road, whether it is for fun or out of necessity, can be confident that the recipes in this book are within their capability. Many of the dishes are sufficiently straightforward for the true beginner to 'just get going' without the need for instruction of any kind. I did, and so long as my recipes are clear, you can. You will probably do it considerably better than me.

If you are terrified by the complexity of cookery books as I was only a few years ago, you now have the stepping stones you will need when you launch yourself into the kitchen. You will not find whole page colour pictures of virtually unattainable dishes prepared without regard to cost by this or that celebrity chef. Instead, you will find clear instructions for straightforward, healthy dishes from Britain and France which you can present in your own way at home. Go at your own pace, as indeed I did, into a fascinating new world. Enjoy what you buy, what you grow or even what you shoot and turn it into something that is interesting and fun to eat.

The ingredients in the recipes are those nature has blessed us with and not what the food factories have processed for sale, and you will find that the little twists and turns of delight from Provence which can be woven into good country food will give a great deal of satisfaction. The recipes have been gleaned from a wide range of historical and contemporary sources from England and France. I have adjusted them as necessary and you will find them do-able, economical and healthy. Many of them I have created myself. They have all been tested exhaustively by me in my own kitchen where this book is used every day and where many of the recipes are firm favourites. Above all, you will find nothing which is inherently tricky or needing years of practice. A beginner can start with the easiest recipes and gradually build brick upon brick towards greater things whereas an established cook might find an idea or two.

Those two rustic idylls, the district around the valley of the River Alde in Suffolk, and the countryside of Provence, have been brought together on my own journey of discovery in the world of cooking. I hope you too will share my enthusiasm and enjoy your own cookery journey – from Aldeburgh to Aix-en-Provence.

Above all, I hope you will use this book in your own kitchen as I do in mine.

RA Freeman
Suffolk, 2019

A SUFFOLK MARDLE

If a word such as 'mardle' could be found in the Shorter Oxford English Dictionary the entry might run something like this:

mardle / ma:dl / *n. & v.i. Dial.* (OE moedlan)
1. *v.i.* to chat or gossip 2. *n.* a chat 3. *n.* a village pond.

However, the ultimate authority, The Oxford English Dictionary itself, recognises the East Anglian origin of the word and various meanings, but to those of us brought up in North East Norfolk a 'mardle' has a fairly well defined meaning which remains part of the dialect still extant in both Norfolk and Suffolk, and it is a mardle that I now offer you. The purpose of this particular mardle is to answer the question I am so often asked, which is why I became interested in food and cooking and what inspired me to try to teach myself to cook.

Curiously, or perhaps not so curiously, the story is inextricably linked with a fascination with wine, and yet the very first experience which created a deep and lasting impression was not one of wine but one of French gastronomy, and in particular the true gastronomy of Provence.

Before I went to university I took a gap year, unfashionable in those days, and during that time I had a job at a food factory in the French Alps. I have many happy memories of my stay there, amongst them being three memorable experiences which might amuse you.

During my time at the factory I had a number of different tasks, one of which was to work with a commercial traveller. He operated in and around the Haute Savoie, but occasionally went further afield and sometimes as far as the Midi. I remember being delighted to hear one week that we were going to Marseille, a trip which would take several days. We visited seemingly every small grocer's shop in the Basses Alpes on that journey, village by village as the road wound on. We checked their stock of our products, made sure that they were not being ruined in the window displays by the ultra violet from the strong late spring sunshine and took more orders wherever we could.

The drive was sensational. We had taken La Route Napoleon which was much more uncomfortable in those days. The bends were everlasting, the road narrow and tortuous, the drops horrific as we climbed, and the surface poor. The salesman's car was a pale blue Simca Aronde, a good French saloon car of its day which went splendidly and cornered well in his capable hands. I remember especially the way he threw the car round the bends, the Michelin 'X' tyres wailing with the speed and heat. I was impressed! French driving was pretty sporting compared with the staid motoring I knew at home. The noise of the tyres, the brakes, the straining engines and the almost continuous blowing of *klaxons* suited the Latin temperament.

A strong memory of that trip was the characteristic odoriferous greeting of the grocery shops we visited. Imagine an amalgam of soap powder, overripe melons, fruit and vegetables in a hot and sticky small shop, the kind of shop where the chocolate bars had melted in their silver foil and where only well packaged goods which were kept out of the sunlight had a chance. Our food products kept in pretty good condition in their industrially produced silver foil packaging, but I do remember having to check the sell–by dates, the first experience I had ever had of such things, occasionally opening a packet to sniff, taste and ensure that all was in order. And then of course there were the interminable discussions with the inevitably white aproned patron followed by the obligatory glass of rouge for the road. I was usually excused the alcohol, and became fond of a most refreshing glass of vivid green *menthe a l'eau*. Poor English boy! He was, thankfully, not expected to take the pace!

As we drove through the mountains and closer to the shores of the Mediterranean the red wine gave way to *pastis*, although I do seem to remember I was allowed to stick to my refreshing mint which is wonderfully good in the heat.

The journey continued and after many kilometres in the Basses Alpes, La Route Napoleon began to drop down towards Cannes, but we needed to leave the noble general's path and take the road westwards towards Marseille. That great city eventually came into sight in a distant blue haze and with it the prospect of good food and a rest from the heat of the road, and it was in Marseille that I was taken to eat my very first *bouillabaisse*, that zenith of Provençal cooking.

I can still see the bowl of strange fish and soup in front of me, in a dark little restaurant in the depths of Marseille. I remember, too, not knowing quite how to manage it, and having to be told to spread the *rouille* on the garlic impregnated *croutons* and float them in the soup. What I do know is that this memory means that any opportunity to enjoy a *bouillabaisse* is never missed when I'm in the South of France. The recipe for *bouillabaisse* seems subject to infinite variation and very much reflects the style of the person who made it, although there is, apparently, an official authentic version but I doubt whether anyone sticks to it. The dish is, of course, dependent upon what fish is available in the market that day although *rascasse*, the spiny headed scorpion fish prolific in the Northern Mediterranean, is regarded as an essential ingredient. In Provence, sardine and cod *bouillabaisses* are frequently made.

Another experience I would like to relate is my first taste of *pastis*, that powerful refreshment so beloved by the players of *boules* and so strongly suggestive of the sun drenched villages of the South. I have come to think of this experience as my *pastis* lesson. On reflection I think everyone should have one, although the lesson I shall relate was not given by an old man in a moment of relaxation during play on a hot afternoon but by someone born and bred in the Haute Savoie, that region of hills and forests many kilometres North towards the Swiss border. I tell you that because I can only surmise, that a *pastis* lesson given under the shade of the plane trees during a break in play, a moment normally filled with a torrent of views about the iniquities of one's opponents, would be somewhat different.

My tutor in *pastis*, Louis, was the manager of the *"temps et methodes"* department in the factory where I worked. He loved to walk in the hills and often used to talk of the wonders of the wild mountain strawberries. My *pastis* lesson came on a walk when I accompanied him to search for strawberries in the Alpine foothills above Grenoble on a beautiful early summer morning. The walking was not easy. I remember one had to pick one's way through the stony but fern covered forest floor and I am sure I was very glad to stop for a moment when we sat down to rest by the side of a rushing rill wending its way down from the Alps, disgorging a never-ending stream of crystal clarity.

As he sat down, Louis pulled a container roughly equivalent in size to an Englishman's brandy flask from the depths of his rucksack, together with two small, thick glasses into which he poured a measure of *pastis,* a seemingly innocuous yet strong alcoholic aniseed drink beloved by so many true Frenchmen. Hallucinatory it may be, perilous even, yet attractive in the sunlight shafting through the trees. As he held each glass under the cascade of water milky clouds appeared. Studying them carefully and then tasting with evident pleasure he said: "that is the way – the only way – to drink *pastis*".

On my last day at the factory, where everyone had been most patient with my attempts to grasp the language and where I am sure I could not have been remotely useful, I hosted a lunch for my boss and three of his colleagues at a good local restaurant which boasted a Michelin star. When I went there in advance to book the table and settle the menu I particularly remember that when it came to the wines I was completely stumped and so, on my return to work I sought the advice of my boss, a French aristocrat of the old school. He was a man of some style and drove a Triumph TR4. To have an English sports car in France in the 1960s was pretty cool, and as I had expected, he knew his wines well. He suggested that a 1959 Gewurtztraminer (sic) and a Beaujolais would complement the menu I had chosen, and those were the wines we had. Perhaps it was with considerable prescience, when inscribing the menu which I still possess to this day, part of his inscription read:

"Au plus Français des Anglais je souhaite de ne pas trop vite oublier le goût du Gewurtztraminer et du Beaujolais" – to this very French of Englishmen I hope the taste of the Gewurtztraminer and the Beaujolais will not too quickly be forgotten.

I suppose that was really my very first wine memory, but I have an amusing tale of wine from England you might enjoy.

I lived in those days with my parents in rural Norfolk in an ancient farmhouse with a large cellar and I always remember thinking what a pity it was empty. I was therefore delighted to hear one day that a French friend of my father had despatched some wine to us. Imagine my surprise, and my father's too, when a barrel of Beaujolais arrived at the house on the back of the local, extremely well used if not to say somewhat dog-eared, British Railways delivery lorry. Our country railway station employed only one ticket clerk and one driver, but no driver's mate, so the unfortunate fellow had to unload the enormously heavy barrel by himself with only a long plank of wood to help. His only choice was to roll the barrel from the tailboard to the ground, hoping that he would be able to control it as it descended, but unfortunately gravity grabbed hold of the reins. The barrel trundled earthwards with increasing speed and then swung sideways in one deft movement like a weathervane on a blustery day, hitting the gravel with a crunch and continuing on its way, uncontrollably and unstoppably in charge of its own destiny. Rolling down the slope of the drive it continued quite some way, only to be brought to a halt against the brickwall of a nearby barn with that sickening sort of crunch that people in charge of barrels must dread. Then it started to seep. The seep turned to a trickle. That deep purple liquid emerging from old oak is a sight I shall never forget, but the trickle did not last too long. Happily the damage was not catastrophic, and the contents were bottled by a Norwich vintner the following day. The wine had been saved.

My next memory of wine is not until I was working in London some years later when my boss called me in and said that the firm would like me to go to work in the Paris office. Perhaps he thought I needed convincing, although I doubt that I did. He spoke of the many advantages of living in Paris which he had much enjoyed when he had lived there a few years earlier. Amongst them, he said, was the fact that wine was cheap, which in those days it was.

To live in Paris at some point in one's life is without doubt an extraordinary experience. To be surrounded by the life of the most magical city in the world subconsciously creates an awareness of aesthetic values relating to so very many different aspects of life. That awareness may lie latent for years and may only begin to emerge into one's own consciousness as understanding grows. No matter how or when one is affected by this intense experience the feelings remain in permanence, and the sights, sounds, smells and happenings of every day stay as fresh as if they were those of yesterday. I was intrigued to discover only recently that Ernest Hemingway, one of the great writers of the C20 said, "if you are lucky enough to have lived in Paris as a young man then, wherever you go for the rest of your life, it stays with you, for Paris is a moveable feast". As one such young man I count myself extremely lucky.

International business of that era thrived in Paris on long discussions over lunch, and sometimes over dinner. My own firm had a pragmatic approach to entertaining its guests, keeping an apartment in Paris for that purpose. It was on the ground floor of a magnificent house in a grandiose and impressive street only a stone's throw from The Elysée Palace. The apartment was just as one might expect in a building of that stature, the walls elegantly decorated throughout with fabrics of French design and a comfortably furnished salon. The elderly Portuguese housekeeper cared admirably for all the guests who stayed or ate there and, as could be expected, the lunches and dinners she prepared were excellent in a Southern European style.

My firm had adopted a rather clever policy on wine. One has to remember that this was in the seventies, when life was less complicated and before we had all been exposed on both sides of the Channel to the pretentiousness of the wine writers and all the modern day wine snobbery that goes with it. Happily, phrases created by the wine tasters like 'hints of boysenberry and fruitcake pump through the briar edged finish' were unknown, yet alone 'notes of crushed black cherry accented by details of ground ginger and anise that ride the creamy mousse showing hints of candied kumquat and brioche, long and vibrant with a snappy mineral tinged finish'! The policy was simple. Claret was served and claret it was. For most guests a good Bordeaux from a highly reputable shipper was provided, but for the more influential visitors an excellent Medoc from a bourgeois chateau was brought to the table. That chateau has prospered over the years and now makes an excellent wine at an affordable price, notwithstanding the ever burgeoning cost of the grander wines from Bordeaux. Nowadays the classed growths of Bordeaux and even many of the bourgeois chateaux command idiotic prices, the flames being fanned by the prosperous middle classes in industrial Asia. Genuine lovers of wine without bottomless purses are now being forced to look elsewhere.

All that was the grander side of Parisian life, and it should not overshadow the importance of the everyday gatherings of colleagues. The cheapest of small restaurants local to the office with a décor of mirrors and bright green paint, and equipped with plastic check tablecloths, the popular press on a rack and hideously noisy coffee machines were regular haunts, but even in those modest establishments the food and wine interested everyone. The waiters we came to know were always ready to advise on the best dishes of the day and, of course, on the wines which would go with them. I was always intrigued by the fact that the patron's granny, no matter which patron or indeed which granny, or if not granny one or another member of the family possessed a vineyard in some far flung part of France. The families were always huge, and there was a certainty that one or other of the enormous reservoir of relations would be able to come up trumps. The wine was usually served in an unlabelled bottle which had undoubtedly followed a circuitous route from the vineyard to Paris in order to avoid the gaze of the various tax officials strategically placed along its way. But the food was always appetising, the polished white plates red hot. This was, of course, the real world and comforting it was too.

These experiences of France at midday – how nice it was that no-one expected *le déjeuner* to be a rushed affair – extended after work into a search for the best value, the choicest foods and the best cheap wines, and I can still see those little shops along my walk home from the office stacked to the ceilings with spicy sausages and groceries to satisfy the gastronome. I shall never forget the appetising smells, too. I particularly remember pressing my nose against the windows of the completely unaffordable *traiteurs,* their windows and cool cabinets crammed with the most staggeringly beautiful foods. I especially fancied *les oeufs en gelées,* a fascination which dated back to my very first visit to France, to Brittany, at the age of nine. Those were the days before the advent of roll-on-roll-off ferries to Cherbourg, and I have never forgotten the look on my father's face as our beloved motor car was hoisted in a sling from the hold of the ship, over the side and on to the quay – safely, I am happy to say. However, the memory of *oeufs en gélees* is equally strong in my mind and I have loved them ever since.

I also have to admit that I succumbed whenever I could to the pleasures of the *pâtissier.* That love dated from my days in Grenoble where, at street level in my apartment block, there was an excellent patisserie shop which sold delicious chocolate eclairs. I just do not understand how the sheer artistry of so many French patisserie shops cannot be emulated in Britain. In every small French town the quality of patisserie will far exceed any of the utterly miserable offerings one sees in the windows of bakeries North of the Channel. Napoleon's military intelligence must have been pretty poor; this fact alone ought to have been enough to put him off any ideas of invasion.

· · · · · · · · · ·

After these wonderful experiences, imagine the distress at being called back to work in the London head office with a view to participating in a growing business activity in Japan. Life would never be the same again.

Nevertheless, my frequent and quite lengthy visits to Japan did open my eyes to a fascinating and wholly contrasting culture. The artistry of Japanese chefs has to be seen to be believed, although their wonderful creations can frequently be found, at a price, in London. What the Japanese do so brilliantly is very largely achieved with an enormous variety of fish which cannot be found in European waters, but the near saturation of fish in one's diet during visits to Japan consolidated an already keen enjoyment of fish at home.

· · · · · · · · · ·

I am now going to wind the reel fast forward again to France, because a mardle is permitted by its very nature to ramble and to last a while, perhaps in the hope – forlorn maybe – that the listener will have the strength to survive to the end.

During a course spread over a two and a half year period at business school in France I was asked one day by a French friend and colleague whether I would like to meet a cousin of his who had a family business making champagne. No doubt this idea sprang from many dinners together, but exactly how or why the subject was broached I cannot recall.

How could such a suggestion be turned down? I am sure few Englishmen would do so, and a visit to his cousin's cellars was arranged. Those cellars turned out to be rather special, being gouged out of the chalk at Châlons-en-Champagne, in those days called Châlons-sur-Marne. Tall and impressive, unlike the much lower cellars of Epernay, they extend several kilometres into the chalk. I remember so well boarding the train at Chalons bound for Paris after the visit laden with free samples, and struggling to throw them into the carriage before the SNCF's allotted stopping time of thirty seconds expired, or was it sixty? However long it was I cannot remember, but how we managed to close the door of that moving train in time I shall never know.

That visit to Epernay was the start of a long involvement with the wine and the people of Champagne and gave birth to a hobby business which lasted a full quarter of a century.

There is perfect symbiosis between wine and food which seems to be rather an obvious observation. However, the enjoyment of lovely wines is the same kind of enjoyment as that from delicious food, and the pleasures of seeing grapes growing in a beautiful vineyard are similar pleasures to those derived from walking an olive grove, or watching a herd of majestic beef cattle or admiring a superb crop of lemons. The magic, and magic it truly is, of a vineyard is there throughout the seasons too. The pruning of vines under leaden skies, or the advent of bud-burst in the spring, carry their own messages. In Champagne, where particular care is taken at pruning time, the cuttings are thrown into those rickety mobile bonfires known as *chariots,* whose swirling plumes of smoke track the progress of the vignerons down the narrow rows and that inimitable and intoxicating smell of burning vine cuttings augurs especially good wine and good food to come.

I sense that this mardle is now drawing to a close but before it does so – and I am most appreciative that you have listened so far – I thought you would be interested to hear about another journey, although neither a journey in cookery nor a journey of mine. It was a journey undertaken in 1784 by a young Frenchman called François de La Rochefoucauld who later became the 8th duc de La Rochefoucauld. He travelled with his brother and his tutor to Suffolk to experience English provincial life, carefully recording his reflections★. I am sure some of his remarks will interest you. The trio took note of all aspects of life in Suffolk, and their observations and comparisons are amusing to read.

On the subject of food he perceived that the English do not eat half as many vegetables as the French, and therefore have small kitchen gardens. He said that the various fruits the English have come from France, and the trees are not very well pruned. He may not have been correct about the origin of fruit trees in general but he was right about the greengage which was bred at Moissac in South West France in the C16 and brought to Suffolk in the C17 and given to the Gage family. This variety was and still is known as Reine-Claude.

He was very unimpressed by our kitchens, which appeared to be extremely clean and well kept where it shows, but otherwise he was shocked by their squalor, especially before dinner. If, he said, you were to find a napkin or dish-cloth or two you would not want to use it for wiping your hands!

Nor was he impressed with our drinking habits. Drinking from the same glass, when there are twenty people round the table, quite horrified him although he did admire our highly polished mahogany tables. He was also appalled by the dreadful port we drank, so dreadful in fact that he was certain that we only drank it because of our favourable trade tariffs with the Portuguese who would otherwise never get rid of it. He also commented that the English consume a "truly enormous" quantity of tea.

François de La Rochefoucauld found dinner immensely boring in England, but not just because of the rigid etiquette. However, I noted that he did not say he disliked the food which seemed to comprise huge joints of meat, and he appeared to be able to eat a great deal of it. He did remark, though, that there were very few stews. This surprised me, given how popular they are nowadays although his observation that sauces were never made in an English kitchen is hardly unexpected.

Whatever our Frenchman may have thought about late eighteenth century English life, times have changed and there is now much interest in good food all around us although for my part, and with hindsight, I should have taught myself to cook many years ago. Perhaps I have been slow to realise that it is the cuisine of Provence that provides that indefinable and inestimable quality of well-being that pleases us all, and that the magic of Suffolk and Provence together have provided the inspiration.

Thank you for listening, my good friend. I think it is time to eat.

À table!

★ *A Frenchman's Year in Suffolk*, 1784 François de La Rochefoucauld. Edited and translated by Norman Scarfe. The Boydell Press Suffolk Records Society Volume XXX

Evening comes earlier

GETTING STARTED

I remember starting to cook with the help of a notebook which I bought in France and which had the rather premature and untimely title 'Repertoire' on the front cover. On the typically French squared paper inside the book I had written three recipes. The first was for red wine sauce which I had gleaned from a French chef, my interpretation of which was hopeless; the second was a recipe (which I have included), for making a skate salad with baby spinach leaves which is delicious and which I had eaten in a restaurant in France; and the third, which I had entered in red ink (no less), was a recipe (which I have not included) for *moules marinière*. That was it. A Repertoire? Hardly! Today, the notebook is full and falling to pieces and will no longer be needed once 'An Englishman's Cookery Journey' reaches the printers.

As soon as I felt I could reliably cook a dish, the recipe found its way into the notebook. Anything that was simple qualified. I started with soups as they are mostly extremely straightforward. Their ingredients follow the seasons, which is a vein which runs right through this book. Stews make excellent starting points for the main course recipes, and if you want to impress, you can say you are preparing a daube! The ingredients can be greatly varied, quantities do not need to be exact, and there is scope for one's own imagination and style without fretting whether the result will look like a food photographer's dream or a diner's nightmare. Cooking times do not have to be precise and the results are usually delicious.

Some of the pudding courses or more specifically the fruits are very simple. Start by just making those dishes which only require preparation, but do not need to be cooked. The compliments you will receive will give much encouragement. Sugared clementines will please the hardest of hearts. Once you feel confident enough to cook something simple, try baked peaches or vanilla apricots.

Using the same technique of 'preparation only', followed by some dishes requiring cooking, try some of the appetisers. The tapenades require no cooking. Those dishes needing a little cooking such as baba ganoush and hummus are good to follow on with.

You might then like to try some light first courses. Cooked cold leeks topped with olive oil and walnuts or a *Salade Niçoise* can be put together very easily.

All these dishes will give pleasure, no doubt at all, and you will feel sufficiently encouraged to progress to other recipes which might take your fancy. Try cooking Mediterranean mushrooms or stuffed peppers, moving on to some of the fish first courses such as Cromer crab with quails' eggs which is easy, or a smoked mackerel for which you could make a gooseberry sauce.

For the main courses try some straightforward roasts or, if you feel inspired, make a marinade and use it to marinate lamb shanks or pork tenderloin before roasting.

As for fish I have found it so very worthwhile to learn about the large number of different species available on the fishmongers' slabs. So many people go to buy fish with cod in mind, look at the rest and go home with cod! I have seen it happen so often. How to cook most of the common species can be found in this book, and many of them benefit from the simplest possible cooking. Baking with a knob of butter is often enough to show off the most magnificent of fish. However, salmon fillets lightly pan-cooked in lemon juice with a little olive oil make an excellent starting point.

So if you really would like to start cooking from scratch there is everything here to enable you to do so. Cooking times and temperatures are noted throughout, although very much subject to the characteristics of different ovens. None seems to be the same, but their idiosyncrasies are quickly learnt with experience. There is also a guide to steer you through the vegetable cooking times.

Make sure your kitchen is well supplied with dried herbs of Provence and organic English dried herbs, and is well endowed with good tomatoes, plenty of garlic (hopefully from France or England and not from the far East), unwaxed lemons, quality wine vinegar, extra virgin olive oil, unsalted French butter, Maldon sea salt, and black peppercorns. You should then be ready for lift off.

As you prepare and cook more and more dishes your confidence will grow. You will want to learn more about animal husbandry, and butchery. Note that there are significant differences between the French cuts and the English.

You will quickly take more interest in fish. That mass of confusingly strange shapes on the fishmonger's slab will translate to tastes and flavours in your mind. You will steer very clear of those dull and sunken-eyed specimens transported from far flung parts of the world, burning up fossil fuels on the way and invariably described as 'fresh'. You will now be looking to see what has been caught on your own doorstep and what it is that provides a livelihood for your local fishermen. You will demand true freshness and sustainability at your table.

I have discovered so much for myself during this journey that I would like to share it now, simply because it brings so much interest, pleasure, fun and wellbeing.

· · · · · · · · · ·

An important message on cooking temperatures

Cooking by Gas

Every possible care has been taken in preparing the recipes to ensure that cooking times are as accurate as possible. The experience of cooking all these dishes time and time again over the past few years proves that the times are perfect for the gas cooker I use.

However, equipment and conditions vary so widely that you may well wish to make your own adjustments to achieve the optimum result to your own taste, and it is only your very own experience, in your own kitchen, which will produce the food you like best.

Cooking by Electricity

The temperature 'Marks' of a gas cooker have been translated throughout into their equivalent in degrees Celsius. These temperatures should be perfectly satisfactory **for a standard electric cooker with a conventional oven**. They have not been designed for a cooker with a fan oven, although cookers and cooking conditions vary, so the cook will have to use his or her own experience to establish the perfect cooking times.

Electric cookers with fan ovens have their own special characteristics, but of these the most important is the **temperature differential** between **fan ovens** and **conventional ovens** without fans. However, the differential is simple to calculate, as fan oven temperatures should be 20 degrees Celsius or thereabouts below those used in a conventional oven without a fan.

Gas Mark	Celsius	Farenheit	
½	120	265	
1	140	290	Cool
2	150	310	
3	160	335	
4	180	350	Medium
5	190	375	
6	200	400	Hot
7	220	425	
8	230	450	Very hot
9	240	470	

THE COLLECTION OF RECIPES

Where do your recipes come from? I have been asked this question frequently whilst writing this book, and I shall attempt to answer it here.

In the process of teaching myself to cook I needed guidance from family, friends, cookery books, newspapers, magazines, the internet, my own mistakes – in fact from every source available – and the generosity in conversation of many people has been a great encouragement and help. What I have managed to glean has given me great pleasure and is encapsulated in the recipes in these pages. I hope it will give you pleasure too.

I do not claim to have written a book of original recipes of my own. It is a true collection resulting from long research and contains thoughts, ideas and recipes from many different sources which start in the C19, traverse the C20 and go up to the very last moments before the deadline for printing this book. Many recipes are traditionally French, and are interpretations of what I have discovered on my travels in France. Others are Suffolk through and through and reflect the way of life in our county. Those I have created afresh have been inspired by the cuisine of Provence, and you will find that all the recipes in the book have been fashioned to bring a taste of Suffolk and Provence into your kitchen without difficulty and with a minimum of fuss and expense.

I have tried to be conscious of contemporary taste and ideas, especially regarding diet and well-being. Times change, and what was fashionable or acceptable only a decade or so ago, yet alone half a century ago or in the C19, is not necessarily what the modern world might want. C21 cooks shy away from lengthy lists of ingredients which require costly shopping trips, and their dishes are neither admired nor enjoyed if needlessly fat-laden and calorific. It is simplicity, economy and a constant weather-eye for responsible farming and human well-being that is required.

In the early stages of my journey along the cookery road when almost any recipe appeared terrifying it was important to avoid unnecessary complication and waste as indeed it still is. Many modern recipes that I have come across, especially in glossy magazines and on television, contain such a plethora of ingredients that the cook runs out of time, patience or money, and I have therefore attempted to keep the recipes both do-able and affordable.

To have the right ingredients to hand hardly needs to be said, but I have discovered that there is no better training for creating one's own new dishes than to realise that supper could be a very frugal affair indeed unless something interesting can be crafted from what is readily available. This is especially so if you live in rural England where the nearest village shop is several miles away and probably closed because you arrived one minute after (or often one minute before) the church clock has struck five, your drive having been delayed by a tractor on the way, your own vegetables having been frozen into the ground and your chickens having stopped laying because of the cold weather. It is at moments like that that I hope to be saved by finding a tin of Cassoulet de Castelnaudary when I arrive back home!

Although the ingredients for many of the recipes can generally be found in Britain, the aim has been to inject a little bit of Provence wherever appropriate, and you will find that olive oil, olives, lemons, anchovies, tomatoes, fruit and herbs abound. Fresh foods, conscientiously reared animals and birds, a low consumption of sugars and moderate use of dairy produce is a vein that runs through all the recipes, and it is noted where particular foods bring special benefits such as lower cholesterol or a high level of vitamins.

Fats have been kept to very modest levels, with the exception of olive oil which is a staple requirement and in any case low in cholesterol. Bad fats such as those contained in margarine have been shunned. Again, controversial chemicals such as those used in sweeteners or food colourings have been avoided completely. Industrially processed foods are scarcely mentioned and dairy produce, so beloved of English cooks, has been kept to a minimum. Cream, that delicious yet potentially hazardous ingredient, has been replaced wherever possible by fat free yoghurt, although I have not ventured into the world of English afternoon tea – had I done so cream would certainly not have been replaced there!

This has been a wonderful journey. I now know that when one sets out with a rucksack full of fresh foods from the Alde Valley in Suffolk and ends one's journey in a romantic, sunny land of fruit and honey, of mountain herbs, of olives, of garlic, of vegetables, of cheese and of fish and fruit to stop you in your tracks it is a journey which is truly blessed.

THE WINES

Many of my recipes carry wine suggestions with them. On the whole these suggestions are limited to the main courses. All the wines suggested are from France as might be expected on this particular journey from Aldeburgh to Aix, but that is not to say that delicious wines cannot be found from all over the world.

Autumn vines

The French have for centuries realised the merits of using wine in their cooking as well as the delights of drinking wine with food, thoughts which are incorporated within many of the recipes in this book. It is worthwhile adding that long slow cooking, such as for stews and daubes, will reduce the alcoholic content of a dish down to a minimal amount and also that the wine suggestions I have made to accompany the main courses are envisaged to be for a glass or two to complement the food.

The matching of wine and food is a difficult task, not so much because it is hard to find good matches but because different people have widely differing ideas and tastes. I hope that the suggestions will be useful and at the least will provide a few clues as to the direction in which to go. Most of the wines are easily obtainable in Britain given the wide selections on offer, especially from the best supermarkets. They are almost all modestly priced although I hope you will not feel inhibited about buying a bottle of Pol Roger, Bollinger or Roederer champagne from time to time if your budget allows. For me there is no greater vinous pleasure than that given by champagne. Its peerless attributes have never been better expressed than by the indomitable Madame Lily Bollinger – that wonderful lady whose efforts, through much adversity, made the House of Bollinger into what it is today. She summed it up in the following well known epigram:

"I drink it when I'm happy and when I'm sad. Sometimes I drink it when I'm alone. When I have company I consider it obligatory. I trifle with it if I'm not hungry and drink it when I am. Otherwise I never touch it... unless I'm thirsty."

Many champagnes go beautifully with food, but the cost does mean that such a choice is often not possible. As for other wines the prices of fine claret from the classed growths of Bordeaux as well as Burgundies from the top growers are substantial due to Far Eastern demand, but French winemakers, stimulated by world competition, now produce inexpensive and really lovely wines from many different parts of the country. The selection is so enormous that something suitable at a sensible price, or in fact many suitable bottles, can be found for almost every dish. My wine suggestions are generally modest in price but it is always worthwhile trying to find your own.

The cookery journey which I embarked upon a few years ago was, and remains, an enormous pleasure. One aspect of it is to experience unfamiliar wines, especially those from Provence itself, a large province extending from the Mediterranean northwards into the Alpes-Maritimes and also along the valley of the Rhône for quite some distance. These contrasting geographical areas produce widely differing wines from a dozen or so different grape varieties, many of which are not particularly well-known in Britain. The Provençal winemakers have greatly improved their quality in recent years, realising that sheer quantity is not what is needed in the modern world, and their wines give great enjoyment.

One of the difficulties in buying from any region is the understanding of the label and back label (where there is one). It is beyond the scope of this book to explain the often complex label language in detail, but the official classification is intended to make buying easier for the consumer, and the guide below will at least clear some of the mist when perusing the shelves in supermarkets, wine shops and online.

· · · · · · · · · ·

More wine

The French classification of wine

A new system of official classification came into operation in 2012 and applies to the whole of France. Certain areas such as Bordeaux, Alsace, Champagne, Burgundy and several others have their own classifications in addition, but this short guide is simply to give some help to the buyer anxious to obtain a degree of quality and value for money.

There are three primary tiers of classification;

Appellation d'Origine Controlée (AOC). The Europe-wide equivalent is Appellation d'Origine Protegée (AOP). AOC refers to wines of a particular geographic origin which may be a major wine growing area such as Bordeaux, but may also be a smaller high quality area within Bordeaux (for example Pauillac) or perhaps a tiny area on its own. The respective labels would therefore read Appellation Bordeaux Controlée or Appellation Pauillac Controlée. Each appellation will be regulated as to *terroir*, grape variety, soil type, vinification, quality and authenticity of style and therefore gives assurances not present in the lower tiers of classification. Wines labelled Grand Cru or Premier Cru have different meanings in different areas, although these wines all fall within the AOC category.

IGP-Vin de Pays is the second tier, broadly replacing the previously well known VDQS. The Europe-wide equivalent is IGP, meaning Indication Geographique Protegée. These wines come from a much more extensive area than AOC and are not limited to soil type, although their grape variety is disclosed on the label. Higher yields than for AOC are allowed. Winemakers have a level of stylistic flexibility far in excess of the tight constraints of the AOC classification. Within this classification is a considerable number of sub-divisions covering seven regions of France, the administrative *departements* and 38 zones, for example IGP Vaucluse.

Vin de France is the third tier. This broadly replaces Vin de Table and is the basic category of French wine. It carries with it few assurances, for the wine could well be a mix of regions, transported by tanker and very rough. On the other hand there are some worthy exceptions if you can find them.

Organic production is recognised by the words 'vin biologique' and accompanied by the French logo AB and the European logo and code number of the certifying authority.

APPETISERS

The Appetiser Recipes

These recipes are mostly Mediterranean in origin rather than Provençal, but are so suited to the sunshine, the warmth and the way of life in the South of France that they seem to be the natural introduction to this journey in cookery. Amongst them, however, is the truly Provençal black olive tapenade. It is one of the traditional dishes of the region and one which no traveller should ever miss.

Baba ghanoush (there are various spellings) is a creation of the Levant coast and hummus or hommmos (which is the Arabic word for chickpeas) is truly Middle Eastern. Taramasalata is indigenous to Greece and Turkey but despite the varied origins of these different mezes they are all so much a part of the Mediterranean scene that their origins are purely academic. Taramasalata, however, does vary in its ingredients, notably whether bread is used, or potato. Perhaps the most delicious of all, the tomato tapenade, is just so moreish that any discussion of its origins will be lost in a haze of second or third helpings and so my advice is simple – just enjoy them all.

CANAPÉS

The following suggestions work really well and are always enjoyed. They are all simple to do, and the necessary recipes are in this book.

Although toast can be used as a base, it is often rather filling and much less elegant than good biscuits. Choose the biscuits carefully, because a moist topping will make certain types go soggy long before your guests have arrived.

Good Scottish oatcakes, the miniature variety, are excellent for the drier toppings such as cheese, but for the more moist toppings such as the tapenades try to find those excellent Italian olive oil based small square biscuits, Finestrotti. Otherwise, blinis are very successful.

For the very first offering try a portion of hot or cold Vichysoisse⋆ soup, depending on the weather, served in a ramekin. It is always a nice surprise, although a slight disadvantage is that wineglasses need to be parked for a few minutes while guests drink the soup using a dessert spoon.

Following the soup try:
- Hot smoked honey roast salmon
- Black olive tapenade⋆ topped with half a hard boiled quail's egg
- Tomato tapenade⋆
- Suffolk Blue, or other relatively soft blue cheese topped with half a walnut

Wine suggestions: Ideally, serve champagne made by a top house. Pol Roger Brut would be a perfect choice, balancing Pinot Noir, Pinot Meunier and Chardonnay. For a still white wine; Gewurztraminer, or if a dry wine is preferred a Sauvignon Blanc from Bordeaux or Touraine. For a red wine; a light and refreshing Loire from Anjou, or a Saumur-Champigny. For a rosé, Côtes-de-Provence.

⋆ *Vichysoisse, p.47; Black olive tapenade, p.27; Tomato tapenade, p.30*

BABA GHANOUSH

This is a Middle Eastern condiment which is a strong marriage between aubergine and garlic (both of which are grown in Suffolk), with help for its success by the addition of lemon, tahini and cumin. It is an attractive combination and is always appreciated as an appetiser with a difference.

Baba ghanoush is a moist purée often used before a meal as a spread on dry Italian biscuits or Scottish oatcakes. (If you prefer a simple aubergine purée in the Suffolk style★ just leave out the tahini and cumin, and serve on toast).

Ingredients (Serves 4)
700g of aubergines
garlic, crushed, (say 6 cloves) but according to taste
½ a teaspoon of salt
2 tablespoons of lemon juice
2 tablespoons of tahini (creamed light sesame paste)
½ a teaspoon of cumin
olive oil
Finestrotti biscuits or Arran oatcakes

Prick the aubergines in preparation for grilling, rather like sausages to prevent explosions. Place them under a hot grill and, making sure you turn them from time to time, **grill them** until the skins have blackened all the way round.

Remove them from the heat, let them cool a little, and then **cut** them lengthways so that they are in two long halves. **Scrape the flesh away** from the skin with a tablespoon, and place it in a colander to drain and cool.

Pound the crushed garlic together with the salt to make a paste. Put the cooled aubergine and the paste in a bowl and **add the lemon juice, tahini and the cumin. Blend** all the ingredients together to make a smooth, fluffy purée.

★ *Aubergine purée, p.53*

Bar in Apt

BLACK OLIVE TAPENADE

Tapenade is one of the traditional condiments of Provence, the name being derived from the old Provençal word 'tapeno' meaning capers. Although the ingredients may vary a little, capers are obviously essential, as are anchovies and olives. These ingredients may have been stored in salt or vinegar solutions, and it is well worth while finding those which have been stored in olive oil to avoid unacceptable saltiness or bitterness. Thorough washing is therefore vital.

This recipe will produce a delicious paste to spread on small pieces of toast or Finestrotti.

Ingredients (Serves 4)
10g of capers, carefully washed
100g of black olives, carefully pitted and washed
50g anchovy fillets, carefully washed
3–4 fat garlic cloves, peeled and crushed
½ a lemon, squeezed
olive oil
1 teaspoon of fresh or dried thyme
a small pinch of ground black pepper
a splash of Cognac if you wish

If you have bought pitted olives, chop them to make sure they really are pitted. There is every chance you will find a pit (a stone) or two. Then **soak the capers, anchovies and olives in cold water** and change it several times before drying them to avoid any residual taste of salt or vinegar.

Put all the ingredients together with a few drops of olive oil in a mixing bowl. **Blend everything together** adding further olive oil in order to achieve the consistency you like. The finished tapenade should spread easily on toast or Finestrotti (Italian olive oil biscuits).

Wine suggestion: A rosé from Provence.

HUMMUS

Hummus, a truly Middle Eastern dish, is so much a part of a world in which appetisers, antipasti, hors d'oeuvres, cool vinous relaxation and sunshine play a vital part that it would be churlish to avoid it on the journey from Aldeburgh to Aix-en-Provence. Added to all that is the fact that it is simple and inexpensive to make and is useful in a wide variety of circumstances such as picnics and light lunches as well as in its role as an appetiser.

Ingredients (Serves 4)
200g of organic chick peas, cooked; or one tin
1 good tablespoon of Tahini (creamed light sesame paste)
1 flat teaspoon of cumin
4 fat cloves of garlic, crushed
1 lemon, squeezed
a few drops of olive oil

Soak the chick peas overnight, or for a good 12 hours. The next day **boil** them until they are soft; this takes a long time; even an hour and a half might not be sufficient. **Drain** the chick peas but **keep aside** some of the boiling water.

If you have not the time to do this, or have not planned ahead, use ready cooked chick peas tinned or bottled in water. **Drain** and **wash** them, but **keep aside** some of the water in which they were kept.

Blend the chick peas to make a thickish paste, adding drops of the water you have kept aside to achieve smoothness. Then **add** the crushed garlic, the lemon juice, the Tahini and the cumin. **Stir** very thoroughly by hand adding drops of olive oil so as to create a smooth, spreadable mixture.

Serve on toast, biscuits or oatcakes.

Wine suggestion: A red from Fitou.

TARAMASALATA

This dish has no claim towards any parentage other than Greek, but is so naturally made from the excellent cod available to us in Britain that we could happily purloin it as our own. However, our own it is not! But it is undoubtedly a wonderful appetiser. The recipe below produces a true taramasalata, so very different from the shop bought concoctions which are best avoided, some of which contain fish other than cod.

Cold smoked cod's roe is not difficult to obtain from the good smoke houses, but quantities must be carefully borne in mind as the gross weight of the roe in its skin will produce only 60–65% of usable roe. Broadly speaking, the weight of the skinned roe should be about twice the weight of the bread to be used.

Ingredients (Serves 4)
300–350g gross weight of smoked cod's roe
100g of not very fresh white bread, after trimming off the crusts
4 cloves of garlic, crushed
1 small white onion, chopped
1 lemon, squeezed
a pinch of paprika to serve

Remove the crusts and soak the bread for 10 minutes. Lift the soaked bread from the water and drain, and then **squeeze out** as much of the remaining water as you can. Put the soggy bread in a good sized bowl.

Slice the roe lengthways, and scrape it clean with a spoon and discard the skin. A roe of about 350g will produce around 200g of edible roe. **Add** the roe, the crushed garlic, the onion slices and the lemon juice to the bread in the bowl.

Blend all these ingredients together until smooth. Finally, **stir** the mixture, and if necessary **add** olive oil little by little until a good consistency is achieved. **Sprinkle** with a little paprika before serving.

Wine suggestion: A difficult choice, but try an oaky red from the Côtes-du-Rhône.

TOMATO TAPENADE

This is a traditional Provençal condiment – intense, powerful and delicious yet extremely simple to make. Spread it on an Arran oatcake or a small piece of toasted Woodbridge Tide Mill bread⋆ if you can find it, or on a toasted slice of French baguette. It makes the perfect nibble before dinner on a hot day and is bound to remind you of the South of France. If it doesn't, go on to the internet straightaway and buy a train ticket to Aix-en-Provence before you take another mouthful.

Ingredients (Serves 4)
250g sun dried tomatoes, drained
1 teaspoon of thyme, dried or fresh
1 tablespoon of capers, washed
3 or 4 cloves of garlic, crushed
a pinch of Cayenne pepper
olive oil

Crush the garlic cloves and drain the sun dried tomatoes, and **combine** them with all the other ingredients in a bowl. **Make sure** the capers have been carefully washed to get rid of the salt or vinegar in which they have been stored.

Blend all the ingredients together into a smooth paste, adding olive oil very sparingly in order to achieve the consistency you want. The tapenade should spread smoothly but thickly on an oatcake biscuit, or small pieces of wholemeal toast if you prefer.

Wine suggestion: A well chilled glass of Côtes-de-Provence rosé.

⋆ *Tide Mill bread, p.45*

SOUPS

THE SOUP RECIPES

A few preliminary words about soups might be useful.

I have found that really good soup is extremely straightforward to make although hardly very exciting, but in learning to cook I have found that many ideas for different flavours easily come to mind. And the recipes are all simple to do. These ideas are, of course, driven by the fresh foods available as the seasons pass, and the recipes here do little more than scratch the surface of the possibilities.

The basic principle of soup making is to produce an attractive and wholesome liquid which is neither too thick and heavy nor too thin and watery. However, certain soups which are *consommés* rather than soups are very thin indeed; an example is *aigo boulido**, the garlic soup from Provence. This contrasts with the traditional Provençal *soupe au pistou*, a vegetable soup based on a variety of beans and other vegetables, seasoned with Provençal *pistou*, a condiment made of garlic, olive oil and basil, not dissimilar from Italian pesto.

Stock, often known by its French name *bouillon*, is the basic liquid ingredient of the majority of soups, although in some recipes just water is used. In the past, many home cooks would make their own stock by boiling up cooked or raw bones of all kinds of different meats, fish and poultry. Few modern cooks will do the same, but you will find that the readily obtainable organic stocks in tablet or powdered form are more than up to the job.

I try to produce an attractive liquid whose weightiness suits its ingredients. For this reason a degree of thickening or body sometimes needs to be given to the soup. This is often done by the use of flour, but also by the use of potato, I prefer and consistently use potato, which you will find in many of the recipes in varying amounts. It is worthwhile sticking to the quantities given if the soup is to be of a consistency you like.

In any book there has to be a least-exciting chapter. Well, this is it! But ignore it at your peril! The nights are cold once we are in the Basses Alpes on the way to Aix and the warmth and satisfaction of a well made soup is not something to be without.

---

* *Aigo boulido, p.33*

AIGO BOULIDO (PROVENÇAL GARLIC SOUP)

This is an extremely simple garlic soup which is part of the culinary tradition of Provence. It is said to have wonderful health giving qualities. An old Provençal saying is "*Aigo boulido sauvo la vido*", meaning aigo boulido saves your life.

This soup is really a herbal infusion rather than a soup of substance, but is traditionally bolstered by toast with cheese, or is alternatively served with poached egg. The following gives a choice of three variations. Whichever way you choose, it is simplicity itself to make.

Ingredients (Serves 3)
1 litre of water
6 fat garlic cloves, crushed
1 bay leaf
1 sprig of sage
2 dessertspoons of olive oil
Options: 50g of gruyere, grated; or 3 eggs for poaching

Crush the garlic. **Add** salt and pepper to the water together with the garlic, the bay leaf and the olive oil. **Boil** for 10 minutes.

Remove from the heat and **add** the sage. Then leave all to **infuse** for at least five minutes and then strain.

Option 1: The plain variety
Toast three slices of bread and put one in each soup bowl. Sprinkle the bread with a little olive oil and pour the soup on top.

Option 2: The cheese variety
Having sprinkled the slices of toast with olive oil grate some gruyere on to them before pouring the soup on top.

Option 3: The poached egg variety
Having sprinkled each slice of toast with olive oil, poach one egg per serving in the soup. When poached to your satisfaction, lift the eggs from the soup and place one on each slice of toast. Then pour the soup on top.

ASPARAGUS SOUP

If you drive around East Suffolk in May you could be forgiven for thinking that the whole economy of the county depends upon asparagus. Down every little lane and around every corner there seems to be a sign heralding freshly cut asparagus, and indeed I know one farm shop which more or less sinks under the spears at that time of year. In any event, there is plenty of it for a short time, and very good it is too.

Although this soup is delicious when made with the fleshy spears of the early part of the season, asparagus remains good for soup making even as the season fades when only the thinner and less expensive shoots are left. However, you have to be quick before it has all gone for another year as the season finishes in June.

Ingredients (Serves 3–4)
25 heads of asparagus (50 if thin)
700ml of organic vegetable bouillon (2 heaped teaspoons of powder)
200ml of semi-skimmed milk
1 medium sized white onion, chopped
150g of potato, after having been peeled and diced
a few shavings of Parmesan cheese
seasoning

Wash the asparagus well and **cut off** the tips and put them to one side. **Cut off** the rough ends of the stalk and discard. **Dice** the potato.

Prepare the bouillon and use it to **boil** the remaining centre part of the stalk together with the chopped white onion and the diced potato. When all is soft, sieve to exclude any stringy parts, but retain the bouillon.

Return the bouillon to simmering point and **add** the sieved vegetables and asparagus and season lightly. Now **add** the tips which had been put on one side. **Boil** all the ingredients together until everything is soft. Now **add** the milk and, if needed, a little extra water and bring it all up to boiling point before removing it from the heat. **Blend** into a smooth soup. As you serve, spread a few shavings of the Parmesan on each portion.

BEETROOT SOUP

This is an earthy, unsophisticated country soup. It is the sort of soup you need for lunch after a morning of hard work in the fields or in the garden on a cold, raw, Suffolk day. Deep, deep red, tending to black even, warming and comforting. Locally known as red beet in contrast to sugar beet, acres of which are grown in the county, it is an important crop in every cottage garden. The intensity of colour found in well-grown beetroot must, I suppose, be attributable to our heavy clay land, although other parts of England or France can probably compete. However, what I do know is that those who eat it for the first time may have a terrible fright soon afterwards, thinking that they have a symptom of a serious disease!

Ingredients (Serves 4)
800g of beetroot, after having been cooked, peeled and diced
200g of potato, after having been peeled; diced
1 white onion, roughly chopped
125ml full fat milk
1 litre of vegetable bouillon (3 heaped teaspoons of powder)
1 teaspoon of dried mixed herbs

Boil the beetroot until soft but be careful not to pierce it as it will bleed in the water. The cooking time will depend on size, but allow between 60 and 90 minutes. Small beet will require less time, large ones even longer.

Once it has softened the skin will rub off cleanly between your fingers so long as it is still warm. (Use food preparation gloves). Do the whole of this operation in advance and have the cooked, peeled and diced beetroot ready to use when required.

Prepare the bouillon and **boil** the potatoes and the chopped onion in it until soft. Then **add** the diced beetroot. After a few minutes **add** the herbs. **Simmer** for at least 30 minutes. Add a little boiling water if the soup has become too thick. Then **add** the milk and bring it all back to a brief **simmer and stir** before removing it from the heat. **Blend** thoroughly.

CREAM OF BROCCOLI SOUP

This popular soup makes you feel healthy just by thinking about it, but it has the added advantage of being very simple to make. It is designed for calabrese broccoli, not purple sprouting, but make sure you buy the calabrese when it is fresh and green. As for all cream soups, use full fat milk.

Ingredients (Serves 4)
500g calabrese broccoli, trimmed
1 litre organic vegetable bouillon (3 heaped teaspoons of powder)
200g potato, after having been peeled
250ml full fat milk
1 teaspoon of English herbs
2 tablespoons of olive oil
1 knob of butter
a pinch of salt

Prepare the bouillon. **Peel** the potatoes. **Dice** and rinse them.

Bring the bouillon up to the boil in a large saucepan and **cook** the potato in it. Whilst the potato is cooking, roughly cut up the broccoli and **sweat** it gently in another pan for 5 minutes in the olive oil and butter. Make sure the broccoli does not singe or burn.

Now **add** the broccoli to the bouillon and potatoes and boil everything together until it is soft. This will take about 20 minutes. At this point **add** the herbs and the milk, mix well and **bring back to a simmer**. Season with a little salt and simmer for a few moments.

Remove from the heat. Let it cool a little before **blending** it thoroughly.

CAULIFLOWER AND ROMANESCO SOUP

Just a little bit different, this soup brings together two types of cauliflower, creating a wonderfully creamy soup.

To make it could hardly be simpler, but so long as you like that inimitable cauliflower taste, which always strikes me as being utterly 'vegetable' through and through, it is thoroughly recommendable. The first time I made this soup I was most favourably surprised. It may have been because at long last I had found something nice to make from cauliflower!

Ingredients (Serves 4)
1 cauliflower, cut up and de-stalked
1 romanesco cauliflower, cut up and de-stalked
1 litre of organic vegetable bouillon (3 heaped teaspoons of powder)
3 tablespoons of olive oil
dried English herbs
seasoning

Find a cauliflower and a romanesco of roughly equal size. **Prepare** the bouillon. **Cut** the florets away from the stalks and place in a large saucepan. Now **sweat** the florets for 5 minutes in the olive oil over a gentle heat – do not let anything brown.

Then **add** the florets to the bouillon, plus the herbs, and **boil** until soft. Depending on the size of the cauliflowers the volume of bouillon may have to be increased to reach the desired consistency.

Season and then **blend really thoroughly**. Blending will make an amazingly creamy soup without the addition of any milk.

COCK-A-LEEKIE

Everyone knows that this is a Scottish soup but not everyone knows that the traditional method of using a boiling fowl means that it takes ages to make. No-one knows that the Suffolk version is quicker and easier, more practical and every bit as good. In common with many traditional recipes endless variations seem possible.

Ingredients (Serves 6)
400–500g of leeks, after preparation and thinly sliced into rings
1 medium sized carrot, peeled and thinly sliced
1 chicken breast, skinned
12 prunes, pitted
2 litres of organic chicken stock (5 stock tablets)
a few black peppercorns

Cook the chicken in water for at least one hour. **Add** a few black peppercorns to the cooking water. When the chicken has nearly cooked **prepare** two litres of chicken stock from organic chicken stock tablets.

Cut the leeks into very thin rings, using the white part of the leeks in preference to the green, and thinly slice the carrot.

Add the chicken, leeks and carrot to the stock and **simmer very slowly** for at least an hour. At that point **add** the prunes and bring the soup back to a **simmer** for a couple of minutes. Then **remove** from the heat.

Now take out the chicken and **cut** it into strips. **Return** the chicken, now in strips, to the saucepan and let it all cool for a few minutes before serving.

GREEN PEA AND MINT SOUP

The peace of the Suffolk countryside is shattered for a short while in summer by the pea harvesters and their attendant lorries rushing their loads to the freezer factories. Pea harvesters, like sugar beet harvesters, are noisy monsters intent on making their presence felt. Nevertheless, the harvest which is rushed to the factories is pretty good and extremely convenient for the purposes of making soup. Peas from the garden do have the edge but can be happily reserved for dishes needing greater sophistication. As for the mint, make sure it is fresh and avoid the fibrous stalks which even the blender will have some difficulty with.

There are countless recipes for this soup and there are (as in cooking generally) no hard and fast rules. This is by nature a summer soup, attractive to look at and especially refreshing to eat chilled.

Ingredients (Serves 4)
500g of garden peas, fresh or frozen
2 shallots, chopped
25g of fresh mint, de-stalked and chopped
700ml of organic chicken stock (2 tablets)
20g butter
1 pressed garlic clove
½ a lemon, squeezed
100ml of semi-skimmed milk
seasoning

Prepare the stock from organic chicken stock tablets and bring it to the boil. **Chop the shallots** finely. **Sweat them** in the butter for a few minutes together with the garlic in a large saucepan. **Add** the stock, the peas, and lemon juice. **Simmer** for 20 minutes.

Then **add** the mint, and **simmer** for a further 10 minutes. Then **add** the milk and **stir** well. Season as required and bring it back to a **simmer**. Then remove from the heat and **blend**. It can be served hot or chilled.

LEEK AND POTATO SOUP

This soup is a wonderful winter warmer and is very simple to make from those very Suffolk and rather muddy vegetables: leeks, onions and potatoes. This soup really does remind you of old black Wellingtons encrusted with clumps of heavy Suffolk clay.

Stick to the quantities closely to bring out the best flavours.

Ingredients (Serves 4)
600g of leeks after having been trimmed, cut into short lengths
1 white onion, or 2 shallots, sliced
250g of potatoes, after having been peeled
900ml of organic chicken stock
50g of butter
250ml of semi-skimmed milk
salt

Prepare the chicken stock, using organic stock cubes. Peel and **dice** the potatoes and **immerse** them in the stock which has just boiled. Leave them there while you prepare the onions and leeks, making sure there is no grit left between the leaves of the leeks.

Melt the butter in a large saucepan and **cook** the onion **gently** for five minutes. Do not let it brown. Cut the leeks into short lengths and then **add** them to the saucepan. Ensure that they are well lubricated with the hot butter, and **cook the onions and leeks together**, gently, for the following 5 minutes, stirring them frequently so that nothing gets too hot. After that time **add** the stock and potatoes to the saucepan and bring it all to the boil.

Simmer until all the vegetables are soft. Then **add** the 250ml of semi-skimmed milk, bring it all back to a simmer, season with salt, and then remove from the heat.

Leave the soup for a few minutes and then **blend** to achieve a soft and smooth soup.

MUSHROOM SOUP

A popular, lightweight soup that is a useful standby. That is what I used to say about mushroom soup, writing it off into near oblivion. However, my efforts at playing with the recipe do seem to have borne fruit, and I am now really rather enthusiastic about it. Ensure that it is made from genuinely fresh field mushrooms, or 'flats' as we call them down here. They are so full of character having little in common with the widely available and tasteless fungi masquerading as mushrooms. If the addition of fats and calories is acceptable, the soup can be improved by adding a little fresh single cream.

Ingredients (Serves 4)
about 600g of flat field mushrooms after having been peeled, quartered
1 potato of about 200g after having been peeled, diced
1 medium white onion, chopped
1 litre of organic vegetable bouillon (3 heaped tablespoons of powder)
mixed dried herbs
250ml of full fat milk
olive oil
a little dry cyder

For a cream soup add 100ml of single cream

Peel and quarter the mushrooms. **Simmer** them in a little cyder with some olive oil until soft.

In the meantime **prepare** 1 litre of bouillon. **Boil** the potato in the bouillon and add the onion after 10 minutes. Once the potato and onion are soft **add** the mushrooms and herbs and simmer all together for 15 minutes. Then **add** the milk and bring the soup almost to the boil before removing it from the heat. If you want a cream of mushroom soup **add** the cream at this point. **Blend**.

SIX ONION SOUP

Economical, easy and appetising is how you might describe this soup. Members of the onion family combine to show their charm and sweetness when put together in this somewhat unusual mix. It is a most agreeable surprise to those who have not tried it before. It is well worth while remembering the onion spectacles before preparation starts!

Ingredients (Serves 4)
3 medium sized leeks, cut into chunks
3 medium sized white onions, roughly chopped
3 medium sized red onions, roughly chopped
3 heads of garlic, peeled
3 shallots, torpedo shaped or round, roughly chopped
6 spring onions, cut into short lengths
1 litre of organic vegetable bouillon (3 heaped teaspoons of powder)
olive oil

Peel, trim and clean all the ingredients, using mainly the white part of the leeks and spring onions. Ensure that the leeks are free of grit, and that all the papery skins of each of the garlic cloves have been removed. This will require a little patience but should not take more than ten minutes. **Prepare** the vegetable bouillon.

The weight of all the ingredients together, ready for cooking, should be about 800g. There is nothing precise about this recipe, and it can be adjusted in the light of experience and taste.

Sweat all the ingredients together in olive oil in a large saucepan for a few minutes, taking care that nothing burns, and, having prepared the bouillon, pour it into the saucepan. Bring it to the boil and **cook** until everything is soft. **Blend** thoroughly to ensure nothing stringy remains.

Down among the onions

PRAWN AND TOMATO SOUP

This soup provides a refreshing and balanced combination between the prawns and tomatoes and is not so fishy so as to detract from a fish course which may follow. If you can, use English tomatoes for intensity and flavour, and if, and only if, you are striving for total perfection make your fish stock from turbot bones. Most amateur cooks make their stock from fish stock tablets which are more than adequate.

Ingredients (Serves 4)
1 litre of fish stock (3 tablets)
175g of shelled prawns
1 kg of tomatoes, to yield about 800g after having been peeled
150g of potato, after having been peeled; diced
1 medium sized white onion, sliced
3 garlic cloves, peeled
1 lemon, squeezed

Peel the tomatoes*. **Prepare** the fish stock from fish stock tablets. **Dice** the potatoes.

In a large **lidded saucepan boil** the diced potatoes in the stock until soft.

In a **larger saucepan sweat** the sliced onion and peeled garlic lightly in olive oil until the onion has slightly discoloured.

Then:

   add the tomatoes to the onion, pour in the lemon juice, warm and **blend**.

   add the stock and potatoes to the tomatoes. **Blend** again and boil briefly.

   add the prawns, bring back to a simmer for a few minutes before **blending** for the last time.

The finished soup will have soft but slightly grainy texture.

---

* *Peeling tomatoes, p.200*

PROVENÇAL COUNTRY SOUP

This thoroughly unsophisticated recipe or something like it can no doubt be found bubbling away throughout Provence most days in the year. No pretensions, nothing fancy. Just good wholesome food. It is best served up at the kitchen table, preferably covered with your best French check table cloth, in large soup bowls in which you submerge great chunks of wholemeal bread in generous portions of soup. Accompany it with apple juice or, if you cannot do without a little dose of Englishness, have a half pint of real ale.

Buy the best wholemeal bread you can find or use the best flour if you make your own bread. For the ultimate in wholemeal flour use the 'Traditional' flour produced by the Woodbridge Tide Mill, the only mill in England using the power of the tides to grind the wheat.

Ingredients (Serves 4)
600g of tomatoes, after having been peeled, roughly chopped
400g of potatoes, after having been peeled, roughly chopped
4 fat garlic cloves, peeled and roughly chopped
1 white onion, roughly chopped
a good bunch of fresh basil
wholemeal bread
seasoning

Peel the tomatoes*, potatoes and onion and **chop** them roughly. **Sweat** the onion in olive oil until it has softened a little, **add** the chopped garlic and **stir** it around. Then **combine** all the ingredients (except the basil) together in a heavy lidded casserole and cover them with water. **Season** with salt and black pepper.

Now **add** half the basil and cook on a very low heat for a couple of hours at least. Three hours is better. Make sure the casserole lid is replaced to prevent evaporation. When the cooking has almost finished **add** the rest of the basil.

Blend to make a smooth soup, but if the soup is too thick **add** boiling water. It is advisable when thinning any soup not to add more than 100ml at a time. **Blend** again to ensure you have the consistency you like.

---

* *Peeling tomatoes, p.200*

TOMATO SOUP

Forget tinned tomato soup once and for all. It is pretty terrible once you have made your own. And think of all that unnecessary salt! However, this genuine, refreshing tomato soup, packed to the gunwales with goodness, is the answer. It is really important to use fresh tomatoes. The taste of tinned tomatoes is quite different and much inferior. A further twist of taste can be the addition of fresh basil, one of the favourite herbs in Provence. Either grow your own or buy it fresh in small pots.

Ingredients (Serves 4)
700g of fresh tomatoes, after having been peeled
1 medium sized white onion, sliced
3 cloves of garlic
1 carrot, peeled and sliced
1 potato of approximately 200g after having been peeled, diced
1 litre of vegetable bouillon (3 heaped teaspoons of powder)
1 large lemon, squeezed
300ml of full fat milk
a pinch of nutmeg
a good handful of fresh basil leaves, if wished

First, **peel*** the tomatoes and put them aside. Then **dice** the potato, **slice** the carrot, garlic and onion and **sweat** them gently in a little butter or olive oil in a saucepan for not more than 10 minutes. Do not let them burn.

Prepare 1 litre of vegetable bouillon, pour it into a large saucepan and **add** the peeled tomatoes over a gentle heat. When the potato, carrot and onion have sweated for their allotted time, **combine** them with the bouillon and tomatoes. **Add** the nutmeg and the lemon juice. Now boil all these ingredients until they are soft. At this point **add** the fresh basil if you wish, and the milk. Bring the whole soup to a **simmer** for a minute or so, but then **remove** it from the heat and allow it to cool.

Blend to make a smooth, creamy soup.

---

* Peeling tomatoes, p.200

VICHYSOISSE

Strictly speaking, Vichysoisse is a cold soup made with potato although the version which is the most common and the most admired is made from leek and potato. However, it varies from the Suffolk leek and potato soup by being thickened with a little cream (although I keep this to a minimum) and also contains twice the weight of potatoes as leeks. It is served cold with fresh chives and is especially good for lunch on a hot summer day.

Vichysoisse was created early in the C20 by a French chef from the Bourbonnais, a region of France famed for copious good eating – I immediately think of the Michelin man – yet it is not a heavy soup at all. Various recipes suggest differing quantities of ingredients. After much experimentation I am happy with my own interpretation.

Ingredients (Serves 4)
250g leeks, white parts only, sliced
500g peeled potatoes, diced
1100 ml of organic chicken stock (2 tablets)
100 ml of single cream or full fat milk
25g butter
Maldon salt

Prepare 1100ml of organic chicken stock. Place the sliced leeks in a large lidded pan with the butter and **sweat** them for 5 minutes but do not let them brown. Then **add** the chicken stock and the diced potatoes. **Season** with Maldon salt to taste.

Cook for about 25 minutes or until the ingredients are soft. **Blend** very thoroughly. Let the soup cool a little and then **stir in** 100ml of single cream or full fat milk. Reheat, but do not let it boil, stirring all the time and as soon as it starts to simmer **remove it** from the heat completely. **Allow** it to cool. Then refrigerate. If served on a very hot day, cool the soup plates as well.

Serve with freshly cut chives snipped with scissors into very small pieces.

WATERCRESS AND TOMATO SOUP

This is one of the very best of all the vegetable soups. Watercress is rich in iron and vitamin C, and this soup's meaty and satisfying character belies its vegetable ingredients. It relies, of course, on very fresh watercress as sold in bunches at greengrocers and in markets. The tired stuff in packets which may be more easily found will not produce the same result at all. Always remove the stalks and any yellow leaves.

Try it with a floating poached egg. It is not only delicious but a meal in itself.

> **Ingredients (Serves 4)**
> 4 or 5 bunches of fresh watercress (a bunch can be as long as a piece of string, of course, but after the stalks have been removed about 200g is ideal).
> 150g of potato, after having been peeled
> 1 litre of organic vegetable bouillon (3 heaped teaspoons of powder)
> 400g of fresh tomatoes, after having been peeled (allow 500g gross weight)
> 50g butter
> a poached egg per serving (optional)

Peel and dice the potatoes. **Prepare** a litre of bouillon. **Simmer** the potatoes in the bouillon until they are soft but beware of losing liquid through evaporation. In the meantime peel the tomatoes*. Once the potatoes are reasonably soft **add** the tomatoes and bring it all back to the **boil**.

Now **melt** the butter in a large saucepan. **Add** the watercress to the butter and toss it about in the saucepan so that the watercress becomes well lubricated and limp. Finally, **bring everything together** by adding the bouillon, tomatoes and potatoes to the watercress and **simmer** until all the ingredients are completely soft. If it is necessary to compensate for evaporation add up to 200ml of boiling water.

Cool. **Blend very thoroughly** to get rid of any stringy pieces.

If you want to add an egg for each person, poach the eggs carefully and slide one into each serving of soup. Fabulous!

---

* *Peeling tomatoes, p.200*

FIRST COURSES

THE FIRST COURSE RECIPES

The first course recipes provide a cross section of ideas all of which are extremely straightforward to prepare and in some cases hardly need any preparation at all. They will not interfere with the effort or the time taken to make the main course whether of fish, meat, poultry or game.

The recipes are quite light and will not upset the balance of the meal as a whole, for there is nothing more off-putting than enjoying the eating but hating the hours of digestion that follow!

The use of excellent fresh produce for all the courses is essential, and some dishes are inevitably seasonal. The fish first courses, which are in a chapter of their own, include a number of species including some shellfish.

One of the merits of a lengthy list of first courses is that they also provide possibilities for attractive light lunches, often rapidly prepared. No longer having to exist on the sandwich shop nearest the office, I find that practically anything can be made in less than the time needed to queue, order, pay and go. Importantly, the wide range of seasonal vegetables and freshly grown produce can be used as a basis for all kinds of further ideas which the imaginative cook can try out.

There are true Suffolk dishes and true Provençal ones, but other ideas have just popped up in the course of cooking or from what was available at the time. The recipes are, nevertheless, all in the vein one comes to expect on a journey from Aldeburgh to Aix.

I have made it clear where a recipe is known to have originated in some other place, such as Italy or Greece for example, but if I have been badly caught out and got it all wrong, I am certain someone will point it out for correction in the next edition!

GLOBE ARTICHOKE HEARTS WITH GARDEN PEAS

This is rather an intriguing little first course that I stumbled upon knowing that I had the artichokes, albeit a little past their best, the peas and some rocket. The result was rather appealing. The down side is that to extract artichoke hearts cleanly and without damage requires a careful surgical operation and, like careful surgical operations, it does require patience...

Ingredients (One artichoke per person)
one artichoke per person
1 tablespoon of garden peas per person
rocket
2 lemons, squeezed

Soak the artichokes for twenty minutes or so in salted cold water to remove any bugs. Then **boil** the artichokes in fresh water, with the juice of one lemon added, until they have softened. Test them with a pointed knife after 30 minutes, although large ones will take longer than this to cook. Allow them to drain and cool.

Defoliate the artichokes, which will be easy if they are properly cooked. When you reach the central internal part pull the remaining leaves extremely carefully, and remove the whiskery part from the heart without damaging it.

Boil the peas for a few minutes, and serve the heart, the peas and the rocket leaves arranged attractively together on the plate. Pour the juice of half a small lemon over each serving of peas.

· · · · · · · · · ·

A simpler alternative is to serve the whole cooked artichokes alone but with a mild oil and vinegar dressing. Clip the tips of the outer leaves with scissors before serving.

ARTICHOKE À LA NIÇOISE

In case you had wondered, as indeed I had wondered for a very long time, the choke of an artichoke is the central, hairy and utterly inedible core of this rather extraordinary vegetable. Once the choke has been removed the joys of the artichoke heart are there to be relished, and what joys they are too. Rich in iron and potassium, the artichoke is also reputed to be an aphrodisiac but, whatever its clinical qualities, a well grown cooked artichoke is an undoubted favourite.

This recipe may not strictly be considered to be a true artichoke à la Niçoise, but in any event it is pretty close to it. It has two facets – the leaves with aïoli and the hearts.

Ingredients (Serves 2)
2 good sized artichokes (preferably the Camus grown in Brittany or Britain)
1 lemon, squeezed
concentrated Italian tomato purée
white breadcrumbs
olive oil
aïoli★ (or you could substitute Hill Farm garlic mayonnaise)

Soak the artichokes in cold water for twenty minutes before cooking them in **boiling** water with **most of the lemon juice** until soft. Let them **drain**. **Tear** off the leaves and put them to one side. Carefully **remove** the choke and discard it. **Prise** any rubbish away from the hearts with a teaspoon leaving them pristine. **Prepare** the aïoli★.

Now **prepare** the leaves with a dessertspoon, scraping the flesh from each and every leaf. **Mix** the flesh into a light dressing of aïoli and put to one side.

Then **garnish** the hearts with a good covering of tomato purée, and **sprinkle** them with white breadcrumbs and a splash of lemon juice. **Finish** them with a drop of olive oil before **lightly browning** them under the grill with a few cherry tomatoes of various sizes and colours.

Serve the hearts, together with the flesh of the leaves mixed with aïoli.

★ *Aïoli, p.205*

AUBERGINE PURÉE ON TOAST

This is a very natural alternative to a proper baba ghanoush which incorporates tahini and cumin. It makes a perfect first course to a quiet supper at home being nothing more than an aubergine puréed with olive oil, garlic and lemon. This purée is not only quick and easy to prepare but utterly delicious and has now become a firm favourite in the household.

Ingredients (Serves 4)
700g of aubergines
1 tablespoon of good olive oil
3 or 4 garlic cloves, crushed
1 large lemon, squeezed
fresh country bread

Prick the aubergines (as you would a sausage) and **grill** them under a high heat until the skins become well blackened all the way round. (The objective is to cook fully the fleshy interior). Allow them to **cool** a little, and then **slit** the aubergines lengthways so that they open into two halves. Using a tablespoon, remove the flesh from the skins with a **scraping** motion. The skin can then be discarded.

Drain the flesh for about ten minutes before putting it into a mixing bowl and then **adding** the lemon juice, olive oil and crushed garlic. **Stir** these ingredients together ready for blending.

Making sure any excess liquid is **drained** off, **blend** thoroughly into a smooth purée and serve on hot toast.

ASPARAGUS WITH SOFT BOILED EGG

The asparagus season in Suffolk runs from the latter days of April throughout May and traditionally finishes at the summer solstice. Whether there is a little too much hype surrounding asparagus I am not sure, but it is certainly very enjoyable when the spears are nicely fat and juicy and, of course, really freshly cut. They lose their brilliance very quickly after cutting. Once the season fades, however, asparagus becomes mean and stringy, but before it becomes too thin and miserable it can be very satisfactorily used for making soup*.

Cooking asparagus does not have to be the ritual of yester-year. A very simple procedure will suffice, preferably by using a standard vegetable steamer.

Ingredients (Serves 2)
16 spears of fleshy asparagus
2 bantam eggs (or small chicken eggs)
olive oil
a few pine nuts
black pepper

Trim and discard the stalky ends off the asparagus.

Steam for 7 minutes. Vary this if the spears are particularly thick or thin. If you do not have a steamer plunge into boiling water for a similar length of time, but check to ensure the asparagus does not remain too hard or become too soft

While the asparagus is cooking, **boil** the eggs for about 5 minutes.

Peel the eggs, place a portion of asparagus on each plate and **drizzle** with olive oil. Remove a small slice from the top of each egg and place the egg upright against the asparagus making sure the yolk does not spill out.

Sprinkle with pine nuts and season with a little black pepper.

---

* *Asparagus soup, p.34*

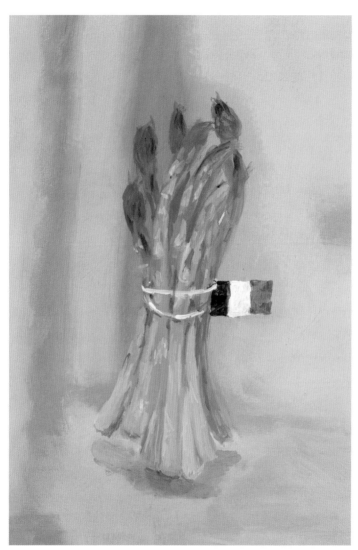

Asparagus

AVOCADO VINAIGRETTE

To judge reliably the ripeness and readiness of an avocado pear is difficult, and practice does not make perfect. Not for me, anyway. However, you should not trip up too often if you become a regular buyer although we can all get that sinking feeling when opening up an unpleasant soapy mass which appeared to have such promise or a bullet-like fruit that never ripened and never will. A little 'give' in the skin when gently squeezed is always encouraging.

Ingredients (Serves 2)
1 perfect avocado (one avocado per person if hungry or greedy)

For the dressing:
olive oil, wine vinegar and Dijon mustard; or
olive oil, lemon juice and black pepper.

Cut the avocado in half, lengthways, **twist** the two halves to separate them cleanly and carefully **remove** the stone.

Make up the dressing in the proportions which most appeal to you. As a guide, one part of vinegar, three parts of olive oil and half a teaspoon of Dijon mustard will work well, but the mixture needs to be beaten vigorously with a fork to attain homogeneousness.

BEETROOT AND GOAT'S CHEESE

Delicious and deep red, beetroot is not that dull old root vegetable that it is generally thought to be. Beetroot and goat's cheese is a dish that shouts 'Suffolk' at you! The aesthetic objective of beetroot and goat's cheese is to build up a little red and white stack on each plate. If the stack building does not go too well, don't worry because the combination of goat's cheese and beetroot is delicious, and it looks pretty too, but there is another method (described below) which produces quite a sophisticated look.

Ingredients (Serves 2)
2 medium sized beetroots
an adequate portion of goat's cheese
2 sprigs of crinkly parsley
a few pine nuts
olive oil

Boil the beetroot until soft but try not to pierce it as it will bleed in the water. Allow 60 to 90 minutes, perhaps even longer.

Skin the beetroot★, and cut each half into slices as thinly as possible.

Now, having a number of round slices of beetroot of different sizes available, **cut** the goat's roll into thin slices, and use them to **build up** a sandwich stack of beetroot and cheese on each plate.

If you find the round slices do not match each other very well, there is an alternative method which can be rather wasteful unless the cook eats the trimmings. I find that quite fun! The method is to match the slices as best you can but then to **trim** the finished stack cleanly with a **sharp** knife so that it comes out as a perfectly constructed duotone cube, rather like a liquorice allsort.

Decorate with the parsley and a sprinkling of pine nuts. Make a puddle of olive oil on each plate and serve.

★ *Skinning beetroot, p.35*

BLACK OLIVE TAPENADE WITH EGG

This first course, or perhaps just an appetiser at any time of the day or evening, is all about Provence and it takes little imagination to believe – a glass of Côtes-de-Provence rosé helps a lot – that you might be enjoying it at the Café Les Deux Garçons in Aix-en-Provence, watching the incomparable sights of the Cours Mirabeau as they promenade in a way that only Southern Europeans can, or maybe you see yourself lunching at one of the many open air restaurants. Perhaps it is one of those dishes that stirs the imagination wherever you are, but it is so very Provençal, needing sunshine, or at least a hot and balmy evening, to go with it.

Ingredients (Serves 4)
4 tablespoons of black olive tapenade
2 small eggs, boiled for about 8 minutes
(or 6 quails' eggs boiled for 3 minutes)
8 black olives for decoration, pitted and washed
8 anchovy fillets, washed

Prepare a black olive tapenade using the recipe in this book★.

Boil 2 small eggs, so that they are lightly hard boiled, the yolks still a little viscous – about 8 minutes will be sufficient – and cut them in half lengthwise.

Ensure that the olives and anchovies are **well washed** and are free of any residual taste of salt or vinegar in which they may have been bottled or tinned.

On each plate make a bed of tapenade and place half an egg on top, sunny side up. **Decorate** each plate with 2 black olives and 2 anchovy fillets.

For a light lunch double-up all the ingredients.

★ *Black olive tapenade, p.27*

CHERRY TOMATOES BAKED IN EGGS

This looks rather like an impressive miniature soufflé when cooked, and those not involved in the cooking may well think it would be exceptionally difficult to make. However, it is very easy and I was rather pleased to have stumbled across it in France. I make it often and the method has been finely tuned. It makes an excellent first course or a light lunch (perhaps doubled) with a difference.

Ingredients (Serves 2)
12 cherry tomatoes, whole
2 small eggs
80ml (precisely) of milk
olive oil
seasoning
chives, chopped very finely
baby spinach leaves

Preheat the oven to Gas 6, 200C.

Cram six whole cherry tomatoes into each ramekin. (Six will fit into a standard sized ramekin if they are true cherry tomatoes). **Pour** a teaspoon of olive oil into each ramekin over the tomatoes, put the ramekins in the oven and **bake** for 20 minutes.

In the meantime **mix** the eggs and milk well together, **add** the chives, **season** with a very little salt and finely ground pepper and **stir**.

After the 20 minutes **remove** the ramekins from the oven and **fill** them to the brim with the egg mixture. You should find that the quantity will be exactly right. (If you are cooking for more than two people you must stick precisely to the proportions).

Return the filled ramekins to the oven and **bake** for a further 18 minutes. When cooked the mixture will have risen like a little soufflé. It will rapidly sink on cooling as any soufflé does. To turn the ramekins out cleanly, loosen round the edge with a knife. Serve on a bed of baby spinach leaves.

BAKED EGGS
(OEUFS EN COCOTTE)

When you fancy an egg and a bit of cheese this is your answer – quick, easy, delicious, nutritious and a perfect first course. *Oeufs en cocotte* is a classic French idea, but if you would like to try it with a little taste of Suffolk, use Suffolk Gold cheese which is admirably suited and quite delicious.

Ingredients (Serves 2)
2 fresh free range organic eggs
a small hunk of hard or semi-hard cheese, grated

Preheat the oven to Gas 6, 200C, and ensure that it is fully up to temperature.

The idea of this dish is to bake an egg in a small porcelain dish and to cover it in grated cheese which melts during the bake. This is best achieved by using a round porcelain ramekin (like a miniature soufflé dish) which is attractive enough to have on the table.

The cheese to use is a matter of personal preference. A relatively hard cheese that can be grated is necessary, and cheddar is often used, but do try it with the semi-hard Suffolk Gold as suggested above.

First, butter the ramekins lightly. Then **break an egg** whole directly into each ramekin, and season with one twist of the pepper mill.

Now **grate** the cheese and cover each egg, both yolk and white, to the thickness you like and **bake**.

I find that in my oven a bake for 11 to 12 minutes on the top shelf achieves the objective of a well set white but runny yolk. Only experience of your own oven will ensure that your cooking time is correct. All ovens are different, and **this dish is extremely sensitive to the cooking time**. You will soon find the ideal, but in searching for it make sure the same oven shelf is used and the eggs you use are always at the same temperature.

POACHED EGG ON A BED OF AUBERGINE AND TOMATO

This dish makes an excellent first course but is also very attractive as a light lunch for which it needs a larger portion of aubergine and tomato as well as some white breadcrumbs to add more substance. It contains the prime ingredients of the Provençal cooking style: olive oil, tomatoes and garlic, as well as black olives and lemon juice.

Ingredients (Serves 3–4)
1 fair sized aubergine, sliced into rings of about 1 centimetre.
500g of ripe tomatoes (600g gross) after having been peeled and chopped
3 garlic cloves, crushed
1 lemon, squeezed
1 onion (or 2 small shallots) finely chopped
a handful of black olives, pitted and chopped
1 egg per serving

Preheat the oven to Gas 1, 140C.

Prepare the tomato sauce first. Peel the tomatoes★, and then chop them. Now chop the onion and olives very finely and crush the garlic cloves. Cover the base of a saucepan with olive oil and cook the onion **very gently** until it discolours and softens. Then **add** the chopped tomatoes and olives and the crushed garlic plus the lemon juice. **Stir** the mixture frequently over a gentle heat for a good 20 minutes, allowing it to simmer so that it thickens a little.

While the sauce is simmering **prepare** the aubergine. Slice it – not too thickly – and **plunge** the slices into a saucepan of boiling water. **Boil** them in a lively manner for about **four** minutes. Now **drain** them thoroughly, allow them to cool and then lay them out on a lightly oiled baking tray.

So long as the sauce has thickened a little, **spoon** it over the aubergine slices. Season lightly. If you are adding breadcrumbs (see above) **sprinkle** them over the sauce covered slices, and finish them with a drop of olive oil. **Bake** in the cool oven for about 40 minutes. **Poach** the eggs to be ready with the aubergine and tomato, placing one egg on top of each serving.

★ *Peeling tomatoes, p.200*

LEEKS TOPPED WITH WALNUTS

This is the simplest of everyday first courses which is always pleasing. Cold cooked leeks were often served at lunchtime in the little café round the corner from my office in Paris. They met our more than modest budget, which was extremely little, and were always refreshing and really rather tasty with a well made vinaigrette. If you top them with walnuts, using halves if you are skilful, you will find the combination of flavours enticing.

Try to find a friend with a walnut tree if you do not have one yourself – they take many years before they fruit for the first time – and collect the walnuts 'wet' and use them the following year.

Ingredients (Serves 2)
2 good long leeks with plenty of white, cut into short lengths
2 handfuls of walnut halves
vinaigrette★

Trim the leeks, cutting off any root and removing the long green leaves and any grit, so that you finish up with at least a dozen short lengths of firm white leek.

Boil them for about 10 minutes, and then let them **drain** and cool. Arrange the portions on a plate and dot the walnuts around.

Finally, **prepare** a good vinaigrette★ dressing to your taste. Sprinkle it on top or leave it as a puddle on the plate.

★ *Vinaigrette, p.56*

MUSHROOMS WITH LEMON AND THYME

This popular use of mushrooms is based on the culinary technique of *à la grecque* which is applied to Mediterranean dishes cooked in a marinade flavoured with lemon juice and olive oil. Cooking mushrooms this way together with a few herbs makes an excellent light and tasty first course where nothing too heavy is appropriate. It nicely anticipates the course to follow with a delicate herbal character.

Ingredients (Serves 2)
250g of button mushrooms, washed but not peeled
1 small lemon, squeezed
175 ml of water
2 tablespoons of olive oil
1 bay leaf
a small bunch of fresh lemon thyme
seasoning

Mix the water, lemon juice and olive oil together and **bring to the boil** in a lidded saucepan which is large enough to take all the mushrooms.

In the meantime, wash the mushrooms but do not peel them. Tie together some sprigs of fresh thyme. Once the liquids are boiling **add** the mushrooms together with the bay and the thyme. **Season**.

Replace the saucepan lid and **boil** until the mushrooms are reasonably soft, but not for so long that they lose their shape. This will take five or six minutes.

The mushrooms may be served hot or cold, using a little of the juice with each serving.

PARMA HAM WITH FIGS AND LOGANBERRIES

This elegant and sophisticated first course, a long-time classic, is simplicity itself to prepare. The combination of flavours is appetising and charming, and the colours of the ingredients make for a very pretty sight when well presented on the plate. Make sure the ham is sliced wafer-thin.

Ingredients (Serves 2)
2 figs, quartered lengthways
2 thin slices of Parma ham
2 limes
a handful of loganberries (or raspberries)
12 or so mint leaves, freshly picked

This recipe requires nothing at all in the way of cooking, just artistic **presentation**.

For each plate quarter a fig carefully along its length and place the four quarters attractively on a **loosely ruched slice of ham**. **Scatter** the loganberries around and decorate with the mint leaves.

Cut one lime into **wedges** and **halve** the other. Place the wedges, and squeeze the halves, on to each plate.

PEPPERS STUFFED WITH TOMATOES, OLIVES AND ANCHOVIES

This simple, well known and popular dish, said to originate from the Piedmont district of Italy, is so much in tune with the Provençal style, and indeed other parts of the Northern Mediterranean that it naturally falls into this collection.

Yellow or red peppers are particularly recommended as they are so much more comfortably digested than green. They should be well cooked so that they turn out soft rather than crunchy.

Ingredients (Serves 2)
1 red or yellow pepper, halved
2 or 3 ripe tomatoes, chopped
30g of anchovy fillets, chopped
a few black olives, pitted and chopped
2 or 3 cloves of garlic, chopped
butter
olive oil

Preheat the oven to Gas 6, 200C.

Cut the pepper carefully in half, lengthways, and remove the seeds. **Rinse** with cold running water.

Stuff each half with chopped tomatoes, olives and anchovies. Finely **chop** the garlic and distribute it over the stuffing. Finally, **pour** a dessert spoon of olive oil into each and place a knob of butter on top.

Roast for about 55 minutes, but expect the peppers to look a little black along the top edges. They will be none the worse for that.

QUAILS' EGGS AND PARMA HAM

This incredibly easy first course never fails to be enjoyed and is in fact a very good start to any meal. Delicatessen (or most proper butchers) will provide the few ingredients needed although quail keepers sometimes seem to lack long term tenacity and give up after a while. Perhaps the attractions of roasted quails are too much for them or perhaps, like my own quails, they came to a sad and inglorious end. It may just be that the eggs are not sufficiently popular, but that can only be because many people do not know how delicious they are.

Ingredients (Serves 4)
8 (or 12) quails' eggs, hard boiled
4 (or 8) thin slices of Parma ham
12 olives
4 sprigs of flat leaf parsley
olive oil

Boil the quails' eggs. Plunge them in boiling water for three minutes, cool them under the cold tap and peel.

Lay out a slice of Parma ham on each plate. Place the eggs on the ham in line and **roll** the ham over them as if you were rolling a cigar.

Two eggs in one slice of ham is sufficient but if you would like to use three eggs two overlapping slices of ham per plate may be needed. You should finish up with a neat roll of ham on each plate.

Decorate the plate with three black olives and one sprig of parsley, aesthetically placed, together with a small puddle of excellent olive oil and a light sprinkling of ground black pepper from a pepper mill.

RATATOUILLE

This wonderful amalgam of fresh vegetables, so redolent of France and evocative of the French country character, has the enormous advantage of being what you make of it and how you like it. Over time you will perhaps find your own preferred method, no matter what the recipe books say. The recipe here is just one example which I enjoy and which I thoroughly recommend. The dish improves if you keep it a day or two.

It has the merit of being simplicity itself to prepare as well as being very useful. It can only be regarded as totally healthy and contains goodness to the gunwales. What else need one say about it? It is delicious on its own, and brilliant as an accompaniment. Its enticing aromas will bring you swiftly to the table.

Ingredients (Serves 4–6)

3 white onions, chopped	2 egg cups full of tomato purée
1 red onion, chopped	1 coffee cup of olive oil
10 cloves of garlic, finely chopped	1 wine glass (15cl) of robust red wine
3 shallots, chopped	1 dessertspoon of balsamic vinegar
7 fresh tomatoes, chopped	splash of red wine vinegar
1 aubergine, diced into chunks	herbs of Provence
2 courgettes, thickly sliced	black pepper to taste
1 red or yellow pepper, cleaned and chopped	a pinch of salt

Lightly **fry** the chopped onions, shallots and garlic in olive oil in a large, open but lidded pan until they discolour. Ensure they do not burn. **Add** the chopped pepper, then the chopped fresh tomatoes and then the tomato purée. **Stir** well and let all this bubble quietly over a gentle heat for three or four minutes.

After a few minutes more, **add** the thickly sliced courgettes and more olive oil. Leave it all to bubble gently for a short while and then **add** the chunks of aubergine. **Pour** in the red wine, followed by the **splash** of red wine vinegar, and the dessertspoon of balsamic. **Sprinkle** the whole with two generous teaspoons of herbs and then **add** some ground black pepper remembering how powerful it can be. Finally add a pinch of salt.

Stir the mixture thoroughly, **replace the lid on the pan**, and leave it all to bubble very quietly over a low heat, where it should be left for about an hour.

Ratatouille will happily accompany countless dishes, but if you just need a light lunch try it with a poached egg on top. It freezes well.

SALADE NIÇOISE

This hugely useful salad, taking its name from that glory of the Mediterranean coast, Nice, can be used as an accompaniment or as a light lunch depending on what follows, if indeed anything at all. There are no hard and fast rules about its ingredients, and much depends upon what is available and in season. However, it seems that the base was suggested by the great French chef Escoffier, no less, and that it should be of tomatoes, French beans, potatoes, olives, capers and anchovies, with an oil and vinegar dressing. Further additions are often made such as peppers, eggs, gherkins and fresh tuna.

Suggested ingredients (Serves 4)
mixed green salad leaves
5 tomatoes, quartered
French beans, trimmed, cooked and cut into short lengths
8 new potatoes, scrubbed then boiled
black olives, carefully pitted
a handful of capers, washed
30g of anchovy fillets
4 eggs, hard boiled and halved lengthways
4 gherkins, halved
125–150g hot-smoked salmon (use salmon instead of tuna
in the interests of sustainability)

Boil the French beans for 8 minutes. **Boil** the eggs for 8 minutes and leave aside. **Warm** the salmon for 2 minutes in the microwave and then cut it into chunks. **Boil** the potatoes. Over a base of salad leaves, **throw** everything else in apart from the eggs, **pour** on the dressing and **turn** the salad well.

Now **slice** the eggs in half lengthways and place on top of the finished salad for a splash of colour.

FISH

FISH: AN INTRODUCTION

The unfamiliarity of strange creatures of unimaginable shapes and sizes, sliced or skinned, headless or filleted, yet all laid out together for sale on a fishmonger's slab is probably one of the principal reasons why so many people shy away from fish. This unfamiliarity tends all too often to cause fish to be bundled together as if it were just one commodity, while the various red meats are always seen as being quite different from one another. Unfortunately this ignores the significant variations in composition, flavour, texture and nutritious value that the multitude of different fishes offer compared with the handful of red meats we consume.

Before the days of my cookery journey I had inevitably come across many different varieties of fish but with little appreciation as to what they were, where they came from, when they were in season and with no idea at all as to how they might have been cooked. My eyes have now been opened to a whole new world and what I will try to do is to look at buying, cooking and eating from a fresh perspective.

The coast of Provence provides a wonderful variety of fish, but apart from those found both in the Mediterranean and in British waters – a good example is sea bass – this chapter on fish is largely, and inevitably, British in aspect. That does not mean that the cuisine of the South of France has been cast to one side. On the contrary, ideas from Provence have been used to make many of our own fish more interesting for the table.

Despite the fact that fish has provided fertile ground for the vivid imaginations of the professional chefs since the C19, especially for sole for which literally hundreds of recipes are known and recorded, the beauty of fish is its exquisite taste and simplicity. There are thousands of fish recipes in existence, but the very straightforward suggestions that follow can easily be achieved at home from fish available in Britain and will give endless pleasure, added to which are the advantages to health and well-being which are well known.

A complicated cuisine often accompanied by the creation of rich and complex sauces may be left to the professional chefs who will doubtless continue to strive to impress their TV audiences and each other, but the purpose of this chapter is to introduce you to different species which might not all be familiar, using simple recipes and straightforward cooking instructions. The overriding rule is to 'keep it simple' not just because it is easier that way, but because so many fish need nothing more than to be baked with a knob of butter and a pinch of Provençal herbs to bring out the beauty of their natural taste and flavour.

Different fish lend themselves to being cooked in different ways – baking, roasting, grilling, pan frying and poaching – but I have introduced an easy method for each fish mentioned, at least enabling the common varieties to be enjoyed.

The influence of Provence is never far away, and you will find that the use of olives, olive oil, tomatoes, lemons, herbs, garlic and wine abounds in many of the recipes. It may be that some of the Provençal recipes are at their best for sunny days, whereas some of our East Anglian specialities such as herrings and bloaters are more in tune with sombre and windy afternoons in Autumn. A grilled herring suits so well those precious moments of relaxation in front of a cottage fire after a bracing walk on Southwold beach, when the rushing sounds of the surf on the shingle are still ringing in one's ears, and the sight of the waves thrashing incessantly against the groynes, as they have done for centuries past and will do for ever, is still fresh in one's mind.

One word of caution is that every oven is different. My suggestions therefore come with the inevitable caveat that precise cooking times and temperatures should be adjusted according to your own experiences in your own kitchen. Fish is not difficult to cook, and in fact is quite forgiving, although overcooking is to be avoided. The golden rule seems to be 'not too hot and not too long', but the 'Is it Done?' test is always helpful. I frequently use it.

The pages that follow, in a few cases, contain instructions on how to cook different fish which are not recipes in the conventional sense. However, the majority are true recipes which are all easy to follow, easy to do and thoroughly enjoyable. However, before launching out into buying or cooking unfamiliar fish the descriptions given in this chapter may be helpful. A broad outline is given of the nature of the fish themselves, when they are at their best, and which cooking methods are suitable. I very much hope you will find it as useful on your own cookery journey as I did on mine.

The timings and oven temperatures have been continually honed and tested in my own kitchen and I now find them invaluable for my own guidance.

A note on fish sustainability

Stocks of some species in various parts of the world have suffered almost to the point of extinction through over-fishing. Despite the now widespread recognition of this problem there are still a number of major species which remain under a real threat. With almost all fish in danger their sustainability does depend on how and where they were caught; line fishing from day boats in local waters by local fishermen will mean that catches are inevitably modest, in sharp contrast to the damage to fish stocks and the environment associated with trawling. It is vital always to choose your fish from responsible sources and find out as much about its provenance as you can.

THE FISHES EXPLAINED

The Bass and Breams: Sea Bass, and Gilt-headed and Black Breams

Sea Bass (technically the European sea bass) is a remarkable fish. It is one of the most vicious, using its unbelievably sharp spiked dorsal fins for protection and attack. It is known in Provence as *loup de mer* (sea wolf) for good reason. Its built-in body armour is well worth mentioning, because the fishmonger who does not cut off these spikes may well have a customer with painfully shredded fingers. They can easily draw blood!

Although more prolific in the warmer waters of the Mediterranean where it is intensively farmed, especially in Greece and Turkey, sea bass is found off the South and West coasts of Britain and to a lesser extent in the North Sea. It is sensitive to sea temperatures, and as the winter approaches the fish that have ventured further North, some as far as Scandinavia, gravitate towards the warmer waters of the Western Approaches. As they start their return migration after the winter they prepare to spawn which takes place in the early summer.

Sea bass has become a very popular fish and is therefore a profitable farmed crop. The farmed version can be distinguished by its darker colour, its smaller size and a more torpedo-like shape, but its taste is dull by comparison with the wild fish. In a conversation with an experienced North Sea fisherman I found that we agreed that the difference between farmed sea bass and wild sea bass was a greater difference than that between any other wild and farmed fish. Farms harvest their fish when they have reached a certain weight and size which makes restaurant cuisine generally easier to manage, added to which the wild fish is more expensive. The ideal for the amateur cook is to buy larger and more muscular wild fish weighing 800 to 1000g if available. The best will have been line-caught from day boats although, because of great popularity, commercial pressures have reduced stocks to alarming levels and wild sea bass is subject to a variety of fishing restrictions.

A whole sea bass is suited to baking or grilling and poaches well too. Fillets are suited to baking, grilling and pan-frying as well as being good for a barbeque. Bass is quite well-endowed with Omega-3 and Vitamin D. It is at its best in the autumn.

The Sea Breams: There are many varieties of bream although the farmed gilt-head sea bream (which is primarily a Mediterranean fish where it has been commercially fished since Roman times) is the most frequently found on the fishmonger's slab.

Wild gilt-head bream is fairly rare in British waters but the excellent wild black bream, once uncommon in Britain, is becoming better known as rising sea temperatures are improving the catches especially off the Southern and Western coasts of Britain during the summer months. Black bream is found over seagrass beds and rocky and sandy bottoms. The breeding season is in the spring and so this fish is best during the second half of the year.

Bream is a really delicious fish and wonderful if simply baked. Whereas the sea bass has the reputation, the bream is superior in many ways. In England buy black bream in preference to the farmed gilt-headed fish.

Bream can be prepared and very satisfactorily cooked in the same way as sea bass.

The Noble Flatfish: Brill, Halibut and Turbot

Brill and turbot, both left-eyed flatfish, are often spoken of in the same breath, although the highly rated turbot usually wins over brill, its less grand cousin. The two fish are very similar in appearance, but brill is not so wide, somewhat smaller and perhaps a little browner in colour and with scales which the turbot does not have. If a fish could suffer from an inferiority complex brill would do so, especially in the market place where it does not quite command the turbot's lobster-level prices. However, recent trends show the brill to be firmly nudging in the turbot's direction.

Brill frequents sandy environments especially in the South West, the Irish Sea and the Channel, spawning in the late spring in shallow water.

Brill may be cooked by any method. My personal preference when cooking a whole fish is for baking, the skin having first been brushed very lightly with olive oil. Baked fillets are especially good.

Halibut is a deep water bottom-feeder with both eyes looking at you from the same side. An exceptionally large and powerful fish, sometimes huge, it is found in colder waters than turbot or brill, such as the North Atlantic in proximity to Iceland and Greenland, spawning in the early spring in the deep water. Wild halibut is at its best from July onwards, but it is a species which is very much under threat.

It is suitable for all cooking methods, and, interestingly, extremely high in Vitamin D. Halibut steaks are best lightly grilled just with a knob of butter. Otherwise recipes for brill are generally well suited to halibut.

Turbot is generally considered to be one of the very finest of all fish, being nudged only by the salmon out of the top spot. Undoubtedly a very beautiful fish, and one primarily for a special dinner, the turbot excels in the quality of its firm white flesh evidencing the huge muscular power used to satisfy its somewhat idle nature. A very wide almost round flatfish, left-eyed and scale-free, it spends its life in the sand and mud on the seabed waiting for something tasty to come its way.

Turbot, which breeds in the spring, is found around the coasts of Britain, notably in the South West, and is at its best during the summer months, but stocks are low in the winter. It may be sold whole or cut into steaks.

It can be cooked by any method, although it is such a beautiful fish that baking whole on the bone is all it needs so long as it is of a manageable size. Very large specimens are poached in a special turbot kettle. Serve with a wedge of lemon or lime.

Turbot bones are generally considered to make the finest fish stock.

The Cod family: Cod, Haddock and Hake

Cod is a cold water fish with a humungous appetite and one of the best known of all maritime fish. After a period of paucity in the fishing grounds, it has recently become much more readily available as the North Sea stocks have improved a great deal. Cod is generally available throughout the year around Britain and Europe but likes the cooler seas off Scandinavia and Greenland. In the Autumn and Winter it is at its best. The breeding season is in the spring.

Very familiar to customers of fish and chip shops all over the British Isles, cod provides a solid and meaty meal and seems to survive almost any method of cooking. Yet baking is an excellent method. Poaching produces a rather bland, dull result whereas grilling can so easily cause the chunky flesh to flake and dry out. Frying produces – well... fish for chips. The cod recipes in this book do, I think, give the fish a chance to show its value, especially cod brandade which is a particular speciality of Provence. Smoked cod is sometimes available, but I find the wonderful taramasalata made from smoked cods roe much more interesting.

Haddock is another deep-water fish found on both sides of the Atlantic. Important spawning grounds are off Norway and South East Iceland. Because it breeds in the Spring it is at its best during the second half of the year. It is landed at Britain's Northern ports such as Peterhead. It is not found off the Suffolk coast, and it seems that there is not much of it off the Haddock Bank in the North Sea either.

Haddock, high in vitamin B12, is another favourite of the fish and chip shop, but can be rather dull. The cookery writers never seem to enthuse about it. Yet a very fresh fillet of haddock can be delicious if dressed up a little, and I have found that a baked fillet with an anchovy sauce, accompanied by lemon potatoes and Provençal tomatoes, makes a most appetising dish.

Haddock has been smoked for generations, notably in Grimsby and on the East coast of Scotland.

Finnan haddock is cold smoked over peat and is a traditional Scottish product, as is Arbroath haddock which is hot smoked over oak. Arbroath 'smokies' as they are known can be obtained by mail order from the producers. Finnan haddock needs to be cooked. An excellent and easy dish is Finnan haddock and poached egg. Some haddock is dyed to deepen the colour. These fish are best avoided as the dyes are under suspicion on health grounds.

Hake, cod's close cousin, is similar in shape and long and fleshy but found in deep water everywhere between Iceland and Africa. It is unjustifiably underrated in Britain, yet hugely popular in Spain and appreciated in France too. The Spaniards buy large quantities of it and their long distance trawlers thrive on it. It is generally available in Britain but in much smaller quantities than cod, and is at its best during the second half of the year.

It has an extremely attractive creamy nature and a soft texture and bakes beautifully. It is less suitable for grilling. I much prefer it in filleted form rather than cutlets but if you need the fillets to be skinned it is worthwhile asking the fishmonger to do it for you. The flesh will easily tear unless the skinning is done well, and I must say that I have not yet mastered the technique.

Hake is an especially lovely fish. French and Spanish chefs will undoubtedly produce wonderful dishes for you using hake. I very much like hake Provençal which is not difficult to do.

Hake can be hot smoked and when done sensitively is really quite a delicacy.

The Herring family: Herring, Kippers and Bloaters, Sprats, Sardines and Anchovies

Herrings: For those of us brought up on the East coast of Britain, herrings are in our blood. What can be more delicious than a fresh herring? Almost anything you may well reply! But give them a go one afternoon when you are cold and wet after a walk on a rough day by the sea in early winter. They will whet your appetite for dinner later. And those delicious roes...!

The British herring industry has a long history dating back to the Middle Ages. The herring was an important commodity in the time of the Hanseatic League, and so those of us living within reach of Norwich and other cities and towns of the League are unsurprisingly attracted to the North Sea herring (actually a species called the

Atlantic herring) and its smoked derivatives, the kipper and the bloater. The huge drifter fleet which operated from the East coast, starting the season in Scotland and moving South with the shoals of herring, was a notable feature of early C20 fishing. The quantities caught were so great that the stocks became totally fished out. The fish were sold very cheaply and I can remember when a herring cost 6d (equivalent to two and a half pence) which was not so very long ago. Even now, and times have changed, the herring provides low cost food which is appetising and highly nutritious, being particularly strong in Omega-3 and vitamin D. Herrings are at their best in the autumn. The bulk is found in the North Sea and Northern Irish waters.

Herrings are particularly suitable for grilling, and so can be prepared ready for eating in only a few minutes, ideally with English mustard sauce.

Kippers: On the back of the herring industry came the smokehouses for kippers and bloaters. Kippers, which are herrings cleaned, gutted and cold-smoked flat are always in demand and became, and indeed still are, an important element of the traditional British breakfast menu. Hotels and clubs (and even some of our trains if you are lucky) can produce them. It is important to buy those which have been lightly smoked over oak chippings and to avoid those which have been chemically dyed. As kippers are cold-smoked they need to be cooked. They are available for most of the year, but largely because fatter herrings from Norway are frozen, imported and then smoked.

Bloaters: In contrast to kippers, bloaters are cold-smoked whole without having been cleaned and gutted. They therefore need to be cooked and have an altogether more mellow taste. They are a speciality of the East coast but can be difficult to find as the smoke houses tend to produce them from the larger fish available in the autumn.

Sprats, sometimes called Skipper, are popular in the East, although generally common around all the English coasts. High in calories and packed with Omega-3 and vitamins, they make an excellent grilled snack. Their best season is during the three months up to and around Christmas. They are good smoked.

Sardines comprise another element in a diet which includes oily fish. They tend to be thought of as tiny fish caught and canned off the French and Iberian coasts and which are only good for a rather boring salad or on toast. However, the larger sardines found in the Mediterranean or off the South Western extremities of the British Isles, or even occasionally in the North Sea, are delicious when grilled in the Provençal manner.

Due to the high commercial importance of sardines some supermarkets have rebranded them in order to increase sales and it is worth remembering that they might equally well be sold as pilchards, European pilchards or Cornish sardines.

Anchovies are of great interest to the cook, especially cooks interested in the gastronomy of Provence. The intense and strikingly unusual flavour which the anchovy can provide to so many dishes is exceptional, as well as dishes and sauces made from these little fishes themselves. They so naturally fall into the hands of the French cook, being prolific and of high quality in the Bay of Biscay and the Mediterranean, and feature in many of the recipes in this book. They tend to live in huge shoals in the open sea although they spawn closer to the coastlines.

Because so many of them are kept for a while in salt and then canned in olive oil, the British cook need not worry abut seasonality. Full of nutrients and comparatively low on calories, anchovies have practically everything to recommend them. Some of us become crazy about them…

The Mackerel family

Mackerel, that small sleek fish packed with Omega-3 and many desirable nutrients is both delicious and inexpensive. The fish come to Britain in huge shoals in the spring and early summer but migrate to warmer waters to spawn in the autumn. The fastest fish in British waters a mackerel can swim 50 metres in 10 seconds and gets this fleet of foot or perhaps fleet of fin from its cousin the tuna.

The mackerel catch is commercially very important and fresh mackerel is easy to find in the summer months. Mackerel is suited to all methods of cooking and is ideal for an interesting first course or a rapid lunch. Whole fish or fillets are both excellent grilled.

Mackerel makes excellent pate when either smoked or fresh, and is attractive as a whole hot-smoked fish, especially with gooseberry sauce or horseradish.

Tuna is, perhaps surprisingly, a member of the mackerel family, but one which is overfished on a worldwide scale due to its great popularity. Although the appealing chunks of fresh tuna which are generally available do make the most delicious steaks, the stock of tuna has significantly declined, and sustainability is an extremely serious problem. The enjoyment of tuna must naturally be tempered by this background. The outlook for the Atlantic bluefin tuna is especially bleak and The International Commission for the Conservation of the Atlantic Tuna which has responsibility for preserving the species has been criticised for the ineffectiveness of its policies. Consumers can of course help by ensuring the bluefin is avoided and that purchases are limited to other tuna species such as skipjack or yellowfin which have been line-caught on a small scale.

It is worthwhile reflecting for a moment on what a magnificent creation of nature the tuna is. Cruising quite literally thousands of miles, the tuna is designed like a torpedo. Its accelerative ability would put many older cars to shame and it can sprint up to 50 miles per hour or more. I should love to know its 0–50 time! It seems a shame in so many ways to eat such a magnificent creature.

The Plaice and Soles

Plaice is, for me, a particularly lovely and delicate flat fish which is creamy and delicious. It is found around the coasts of Britain, and, in the North Sea, plaice tends to stick to the sandy and muddy attractions of the Dogger Bank and, amusingly, the Haddock Bank off the North East coast. Plaice is a fish which likes to bury itself in the mud just leaving its eyes exposed and thus holding itself ready to snap up tasty morsels as they come along. Not a bad life!

It spawns from late in the year until March, usefully coming into season early in the summer offering a good alternative to the lemon sole whose season then begins to fade. It is at its best for the second half of the year.

Despite the efforts of our fish and chip shops, fillets of plaice are suited to gentle cooking rather than deep-fat frying and are perfect for the simplest of treatment. Few fish reward the cook with such delicacy and succulence. Cooking times are quite sensitive, and many recipes suggest a conservative time followed by an exhortation to ensure the plaice is fully cooked through.

Dover sole, that firm meaty fish with a tough skin and flesh with a silky texture has been a mainstay of top restaurants and London clubs from the early C19, these establishments charging highly for it. It is, of course, a costly fish but small 'Dovers', known as slips, make good individual portions if a full size fish is not needed. Dovers are less good during the spawning season in the spring, being at their best (like so many fish) during the winter. Although found in the deep waters of the East Atlantic they also enjoy the shallower, warmer waters and sandy environment of the South West where they like to spawn. They are found in the North Sea when the water temperature is warmer later in the summer but can be somewhat smaller.

All cooking methods work well for Dovers. They benefit from being very lightly floured and then pan cooked in a mixture of olive oil and lemon juice – so good for flat fish generally – or alternatively lightly grilled with a knob of butter. Dovers are best cleaned and skinned, at least on the dark side, by the fishmonger.

Filleted soles open up a plethora of cooking choices. In the C19 and C20 the great chefs of France, and no doubt beyond, invented vast numbers of 'dishes' for the sole and went on doing so in some kind of gastronomic virility contest. In my pocket copy of Saulnier's Le Repertoire de la Cuisine published originally in 1914 I counted well over 300 recipes for sole, and indeed the great Escoffier himself did not hold back with a hundred or so. I am not sure this competition has yet come to an end. Only a short time ago I read yet another allegedly new recipe in a daily newspaper.

However, complicated cuisine is not what this book is about. Excellent dishes can be enjoyed from the simple techniques described.

Lemon sole, surprisingly, is a different species from Dover sole. It is attractive to the home cook being much less expensive. The texture is much softer, the flesh being more flaky and less cohesive. It is very much a Northern European fish and can be found all around the British Isles living in less sandy conditions than the Dover sole or plaice, but deeper down in a stonier environment. It spawns in the spring and early summer when it is best avoided, but by this time excellent plaice start to become available instead. Lemon sole is at its best during the winter.

Gastronomically, it has much in common with plaice, and the dishes created for lemon sole are not dissimilar and often interchangeable. 'Lemons', as the fishermen call them, are soft and delicate and need the kind of cooking that suits their nature where simplicity is the key. Fillets give more opportunities to the cook, although the whole fish is excellent grilled or baked. Fillets benefit from being very gently baked, lightly pan cooked in olive oil and lemon juice or gently grilled, but if you feel you must venture further the sole is ideal for matching with interesting sauces.

Witch sole is rather like the second wine from the lemon sole chateau, not having quite the same degree of style. It lives on shingly sea-beds in deeper waters and is at its best during the Winter. The cook can happily treat it in exactly the same way as lemon sole but the end result never seems to quite match. Nevertheless, it is a perfectly nice fish to buy.

The Noble Roundfish: Salmon and Sea Trout

Salmon is indeed the king of fish, and a whole wild salmon is the ultimate, albeit expensive, creature to find its way into a private kitchen. However, salmon farming and especially organic salmon farming has improved beyond all measure in recent years and organic farmed salmon is generally extremely good. Nevertheless, nothing approaches the exquisite taste and texture of the wild fish and it remains one of the most wonderful foods on earth.

The habitat of the wild salmon is so well known that there is no merit in rehearsing it here, but it still seems to be true that the very best is found in the Scottish rivers.

It is always a matter of wonderment that a fish which starts its life in the shallows of a Scottish river will migrate into the deeps of the Atlantic only to return to the same river in a few years to spawn at the end of the year in order to create a new generation.

The ubiquitous farmed salmon fillets sold at modest prices make an attractive dish, and the simple recipes I suggest help to make the most of them. Salmon is suited to poaching, grilling, baking or pan cooking in olive oil and lemon juice.

Farmed salmon is also smoked in industrial quantities of varying degrees of quality. Some of the best products are very good, although they cannot match the costly wild salmon smoked over oak or peat. Whereas the cold smoked salmon is produced in thin slices, hot-smoked honey roast salmon is usually sold in the form of steaks.

Sea Trout runs the salmon a very close second in esteem, perhaps too close for the salmon's comfort as it is a really superb fish. Yet a salmon it is not. It is a trout. A brown trout which is born and lives the whole of its life in freshwater is genetically the same fish as a brown trout born in the same place but which has chosen to live its life at sea, thus becoming a sea trout. In fact both the non-migrating brown trout and the brown trout that has migrated to the sea to become a sea trout are both known by the same Latin name, salmo trutta. The sea-going trout develops a delicate pink flesh. Notwithstanding the marine life it has chosen it still returns to freshwater to breed.

Sea trout has a short summer season and is the most wonderful fish for a special summer entertainment. Just dream of that whole poached sea trout which you had requested from the fishmonger and which had been caught to his order, appropriately decorated for your party on a summer Sunday! A true fishmonger will have been closely in touch with the fisherman to find out what the next catch is expected to yield and broadly what the price will be. Catches are small and are made under licence (you will see the yellow numbered tags affixed to each individual fish) and wide fluctuations in price are frequent. What you can be sure of is that the cost of a wild sea trout will be a fraction of the cost of a wild salmon.

To have poached a wild sea trout for friends will be the high point of having read this book, notwithstanding the simplicity of the recipe. Sea trout is also ideally suited to baking.

A Mixed Catch

John Dory, a beautifully flavoured fish with a lovely texture known both for its popularity among chefs and its ugliness, qualities which I do not wish to imply are related! Although found all around the world apart from the Americas, it frequents the British Isles in summer, notably the Channel and the South West.

It is instantly recognisable by its large black spot said to be St. Peter's thumbprint, and by its mean, hideous look.

Its subtle white flesh calls for gentle cooking, and it requires nothing at all save a knob of melted butter to enjoy it, although as with all fish there are many recipes for it, often containing aubergine with which it blends well. Gentle baking is the recommended method. Its flesh constitutes less than half its overall weight.

Monkfish (properly called Anglerfish) is expensive, perhaps because its firm, succulent white meat is not greatly dissimilar in taste and texture from that of lobster. Not so many years ago it was regarded in Britain as being fit only for the cat, but it grew in popularity due to exposure by the TV chefs in the latter part of the C20 who realised its culinary merit. It is a creature of extraordinary ugliness and viciousness too, and so ugly in fact that a whole fish will hardly ever be seen on a fishmonger's slab because no one would ever buy it. It beats John Dory hollow for ugliness. It is very much a predator, and its principal feature is its massive mouth which it uses with lightning speed to snap up whatever interesting comes its way. For all these reasons only its meaty tail attracted the attention of the TV audiences, and it is the readily skinned tail that you will find on the fishmonger's slab. The French nickname it *le crapaud-de-mer* (a sea toad) although its proper French name is *la lotte*.

Monkfish is a deep-water predator primarily found off the South West coasts of Britain and in parts of the Channel and Irish Sea and although is generally available it is at its best during the second half of the year. It is suitable for all methods of cooking. When cooked in lumps it can be rather rubbery in texture and the fillets are better sliced or beaten reasonably flat.

Red Mullet is an exquisitely flavoured fish of a pinky red hue which has had a strong following since the days of the Roman Empire. The Romans particularly valued it, both for its attractive colouring to adorn their aquatic collections in domestic ponds and also as a delicacy for their tables. It is deeply embedded into the gastronomy of France and especially in Marseille, the spiritual home of *bouillabaisse*.

The legendary *bouillabaisse* (a recipe for which is not included in these pages) is perhaps closer to an art form than to anything else. It is a quickly cooked stew of a wide variety of Mediterranean fish although almost always incorporates the scorpion fish (*rascasse*) coupled with the assertive flavours of Provençal cooking. There is no single recipe which has to be followed or particular selection of fish and crustaceans that must be included, although red mullet very often plays a part.

The red mullet enjoys a sandy environment in warm waters, scavenging for shellfish on the seabed. It is fished very actively in the Mediterranean but is also found in the English Channel and southern parts of the North Sea. Its principal season is from May to November. Grilling is an ideal cooking method.

Skate is in fact a ray, of which there are a number of varieties. Some of these are at the limits of sustainability. For the most part it is the thornback (said by fishermen to be relatively plentiful) which is generally caught in the North Sea off the Suffolk coast and which is commonly described as skate. Various species of ray, such as the cuckoo, the blonde, and the spotty are found in other British waters. They provide extremely delicious eating. Shaped more like a modern airborne weapon than a fish, the ray has muscular so-called wings held together by a cartilaginous structure. These wings are traditionally skinned at sea and will be presented ready to eat on the fishmonger's slab.

Skate should not be kept too long before cooking. A North Sea fisherman once told me that a skate should be regarded rather like a pear which may be hard when first picked but will soften and go through a period of ripening until it suddenly goes brown in the centre. Old timers in Suffolk say that you might have to get up in the middle of the night to catch a pear at its best. Although the time scales are different for skate and it will not go brown in the centre, it can certainly go off smelling strongly of ammonia. It is best refrigerated for a couple of days between catch and cooking, but it should not be allowed to reach its characteristic ammoniac stage. A slight smell of ammonia can be removed by soaking the fish in salty water for a couple of hours immediately prior to cooking, but if there is a strong smell the fish should be discarded.

Skate is generally available throughout the year although the spawning period in the early summer should be avoided, and close attention should be given to sustainability. It is a fish which is very much under threat.

Poaching in a simple court bouillon is always successful although pan frying and roasting are also popular.

Shellfish

Shellfish are tricky to buy and not always easy to deal with in the kitchen or at the table, and quite a number of people suffer from allergies from shellfish which can cause considerable distress or worse. Some shellfish are difficult to buy with security and confidence other than from the most reliable fishermen and fishmongers, as knowledge of their habitat, their harvesting and their selection is important as well as the absolutely critical matter of how fresh they are.

The specialised subject of shellfish is outside the scope of this book, with the exception of some simple recipes for prawns, shrimps, crabs and scallops which you can enjoy.

Prawns and shrimps may be bought ready packaged or frozen and present no difficulties. Crabs, in season during the summer and well into the autumn, need to be consumed when they are still very fresh indeed, and when I buy them I like to know that they were landed late on the previous day at the very latest and preferably on the morning of purchase. This means that they are best avoided unless you happen to find yourself close to where they are caught. Scallops, equally, need to be extremely fresh, but a reliable fishmonger will also have ensured that they have been responsibly harvested and supplied to him immediately. They will have been collected by divers and not dredged, dredging being an insensitive way of collecting them, as it damages their environment and makes selection impossible. Scallops are in season during the Winter.

Smoked fish

Some smoked fish are rooted in the culinary traditions of the British Isles, such as haddock and kippers which have been enjoyed for generations. There is a little bit of a trend nowadays to smoke anything just to be different, or so it seems, but I shall stick to the time honoured varieties.

It is important to know whether a fish has been hot- or cold-smoked. Cold smoking does not cook the fish whereas hot smoking does.

Kippers are herrings, cleaned, gutted, 'butterflied' and cold-smoked flat and so need to be cooked. They are widely available and familiar, but it is important to buy those which have been lightly smoked over oak chippings. Those which have been dyed to deepen the colour are definitely to be avoided. The art of kippering has long been practised from the Northumbrian coast down to Suffolk and Essex.

Bloaters are herrings which have not been cleaned and gutted, and which are cold-smoked whole which gives them an altogether more subtle taste. They are a speciality of the East of England but are sometimes difficult to find. Like kippers, they need to be cooked.

Sprats are very small fish which are a speciality of the Suffolk coast although available in other places. When smoked they are smoked hot and ready to eat. Otherwise they are grilled and eaten whole, but preferably without head and tail. They are packed with Omega-3 and vitamin D.

Mackerel, when smoked are smoked hot and are therefore ready to eat They are delicious with either gooseberry sauce or horseradish. Mackerel are especially nutritious. Smoked mackerel pate is delicious.

Haddock – Finnan haddock, a traditional Scottish product, is cold-smoked over peat and thus needs to be cooked. An excellent and easily-prepared dish is Finnan haddock with poached egg. Avoid haddock which has been dyed to brighten or deepen the colour.

'Arbroath smokies' are another long standing Scottish tradition. These are small haddock hot-smoked over oak in pairs with the backbone still intact. Attractive, yet strongly tasting, these can be obtained direct from the producers by mail order or occasionally from the best fishmongers.

Salmon is farmed and cold-smoked in industrial quantities. It is beyond the scope of this book to look into the matter of smoked salmon quality, but smoked farmed salmon is readily available. The less good products are inexpensive.

Smoked wild salmon is available but very costly. It is smoked over oak or peat. Hot-smoked honey roast salmon is also readily available, usually cut into steaks.

Cod is sometimes smoked, but smoked cod's roe is of greater interest being the prime ingredient for taramasalata.

Hake – hot-smoked hake is rather special. (It was included as part of the first course of my wedding breakfast)!

Crevettes and prawns, already cooked, are sometimes cold-smoked for flavour.

· · · · · · · · · ·

The 'Is it Done?' test for Fish

This ugly name, sometimes referred to as the 'Doneness Test' which is equally ugly, makes up in utility what it lacks in elegance. It is a test devised to see whether fish has been properly cooked and it is extremely useful. Fish should never be overcooked as it is pretty unattractive if it is, and so it is always best to cook it so that it is only just cooked all the way through. Fish goes opaque when cooked, but as you cannot see through the flesh without leaving a path of destruction in your wake the 'Is it Done?' test is used by cooks to ensure the fish is served at its best.

Method
Remove the fish from the heat and insert a thin but flat knife blade into the flesh, taking care to pierce it in line with the grain and the bone structure. Leave the knife there for ten seconds, withdraw it and quickly touch the back of your hand with it. If the knife is still cool, further cooking is needed.

Anothwe excellent test of doneness is the state of the skin. If the skin is not easily removed, the fish is not cooked.

Reading the paper between fish

FISH IN FRENCH

I once stayed in Northern France in a small hotel where there was a good kitchen and interesting menus. Fish was regularly featured, but as the patron was keen to set out his menu in English as well as French a number of problems of translation arose. In fact the English menu caused a great deal of difficulty, and I was asked if I might help, especially with the names of the wide variety of fish on offer. I said, of course, that I would try, but it was not at all an easy task and not having been able to solve some of the problems from the dictionary I had in my suitcase, I remember finishing up in the local library in the early days of the internet trying to find answers to some tricky questions. Even the librarian was pretty stumped, and I am not at all sure we had found the right site and the answers may not have been too reliable. Heigh ho!

So to save you from much Googling at your French restaurant table which might well enrage *le patron*, I offer help here in the knowledge that it is more reliable than the answers given all those years ago.

Anchovy. . . . . Anchois *m.*

Black Bream . . . . .Daurade grise *f.*

Brill . . . . Barbue *f.*

Cod (salt Cod) . . Cabillaud *m.* (Morue *f.*)

Crab. . . . . .Crabe *f.*

Haddock. . . . . Aiglefin *m.*

Hake . . . . .Merlu *m.* (in Provence); . . . . Colin *m.* (generally)

Halibut. . . . . .Flétan *m.*

Herring . . . . .Hareng *m.*

John Dory. . . . . St. Pierre *m.*

Lemon Sole. . . . . .Limande *f.*

Lobster . . . . Homard *m.*

Mackerel. . . . . Maquereau *m.*

Monkfish . . . . Lotte *f.*

Mussels. . . . . .Moules *f.*

Oysters. . . . . .Huitres *f.*

Pike . . . . Brochet *m.*

Pike-perch . . . . Sandre *m.*

Prawn. . . . . Crevette rose *f.*

Plaice . . . . Carrelet *m.*

Red Mullet. . . . . .Rouget *m.*

Scallops. . . . . .Coquilles St. Jacques *f.*

Sea Bream. . . . . .Daurade (Dorade) *f.*

Salmon . . . . Saumon *m.*

Sea Bass . . . . Loup de Mer (Bar) *m.*

Sea trout. . . . . .Truite de mer *f.*

Skate . . . . .Raie *f.*

Sole . . . . Sole *f.*

Sprat. . . . . .Sprat / Harenguet *m.*

Trout . . . . Truite *f.*

Turbot . . . . Turbot *m.*

Whitebait . . . . Blanchaille *f.*

FISH FIRST COURSES

ANCHOÏADE (ANCHOYADE)

This is the very essence of Provence, a traditional dish bringing out the intense savours that the combination of anchovy and garlic will produce. These sensations bring back to the traveller the relish of times past, of long hot sunny days spent in seemingly endless sunshine and warm evenings whiled away with good friends. To the native of Provence they will be associated with convivial company and good local rosé in comforting and familiar places. Anchoïade is a potent reminder of the stress free ambience of the South of France.

Ingredients (Serves 2)
50–60g of anchovies, crushed
3 or 4 cloves of garlic, crushed
1 dessertspoon of tomato purée
1 dessertspoon of cognac (optional)
olive oil

The anchovies may have been bottled or tinned in vinegar, salt or vegetable oil. Those which have been in vinegar are best avoided as it is almost impossible to remove the taste of vinegar, no matter how much they are washed. Those in salt need to be washed extremely thoroughly, and so go for those in olive oil whenever possible. Try to find a jar of anchovies from Fish 4 Ever, preserved in extra virgin olive oil.

Preheat the oven to Gas 6, 200C.

Crush the garlic in a pestle and mortar to make a smooth paste, adding a little olive oil to achieve consistency.

Add the anchovies and crush them into the garlic paste.

Add the tomato purée (and cognac) and mix everything together well. **Cut** a few thick slices of country bread and divide them into squares. **Toast** them lightly under the grill on **one side only**. Spread the anchoiade on the untoasted sides and place them in the oven for 3 or 4 minutes.

COD CHEEKS IN A PROVENÇAL STYLE

Cheeky this recipe most certainly is, as I have matched the fish with a Provençal style sauce most presumptuously. Cod cheeks are not especially well known in Britain although are starting to become fashionable, but as the cod is a cold water Atlantic fish that only occasionally ventures into the Mediterranean it does not generally feature in Mediterranean cooking.

A lady from Saxmundham most charmingly observed that the cheeks depend for their size on the breadth of the smile, but whatever their size they look rather like scallops and may be very simply pan-fried in olive oil and lemon juice with a few herbs, or cooked together with black olives and tomatoes in the Provençal manner. Nevertheless, they make a healthy and exceptionally enjoyable dish, whether for a first or main course, the method for which I can claim no authenticity whatsoever, but I am sure it will quickly become a firm favourite. For a main course double the quantities.

Ingredients (Serves 2)
6 to 8 cod cheeks
1 lemon, squeezed
30g anchovies, chopped
garlic olive oil (or olive oil and crushed garlic)
a very good handful of black olives, pitted and chopped
3 good sized tomatoes, chopped
black pepper
herbs of Provence

Cover the base of a wide, lidded pan with garlic olive oil. **Add** the lemon juice and the chopped olives, anchovies and tomatoes. Replace the lid and **cook** over a medium heat for about five minutes until the ingredients have softened.

Add the cod cheeks to the pan, **season** with black pepper and a small pinch of herbs of Provence. Replace the lid and let all the ingredients **simmer** together quietly for approximately 8 minutes by which time the cheeks will have become opaque. Serve with all the cooking juices.

CROMER CRAB AND QUAILS' EGG SALAD

If a dressed crab pure and simple is a little too rich this makes an extremely tasty alternative.

Above all, the crab must be really fresh and of a good size as crabs must be not sold if less than 4 1/2" in breadth. Ideally, crab is best landed no sooner than the previous afternoon and dressed on the morning of purchase. The crab season depends on the temperature of the water and lasts from late Spring until well into the Autumn and finishes very roughly at the time the lobster pots are brought in for the winter.

To turn a dressed crab into an appetising salad is very much a matter of one's own preferences and and so the ingredients of this salad should largely be left to the flair of the cook. The following recipe is a suggestion for a refreshing salad. It can be doubled up if you want to make a lunch dish or a main course.

Ingredients (Serves 2)
1 large fresh dressed crab
2 sweet baby gherkins, very finely diced
2 smallish tomatoes, finely diced
6 quails' eggs, hard boiled★
1 lime, squeezed
1 dessertspoon of olive oil, approximately
a splash of dry white wine

Cook the quails' eggs. **Remove** the dressed crab from its shell and place the meat in a mixing bowl. With a fork **mix** the white and brown meat together adding the lime juice. **Add** the very finely diced gherkins and then do the same with the diced tomatoes. **Mix** thoroughly, **season** and **add** the olive oil slowly to achieve a consistency which will enable the salad to be shaped on the plate as you wish. Halve the eggs lengthways and place them on top of the salad.

Wine suggestion: a Sauvignon blanc from Bordeaux.

★ *Boiling quails' eggs, p.186*

MACKEREL (SMOKED) PÂTÉ

Mackerel provides a welcome shot of Omega-3 and is reputed to have many health giving properties especially for the cardiovascular system. Whatever those may be, it's delicious!

Ensure you find a first class source of good fish and an excellent smoke house. Buy the smoked fish whole. Avoid if possible the flattened, packaged product which is more readily available.

Traditionally, smoked mackerel is accompanied by gooseberries, or otherwise made into a dish using cream of horseradish. The pâté, however, is ideally made with Greek yoghurt as set out in this recipe.

Ingredients (Serves 3–4)
1 whole smoked mackerel
1 tablespoon Greek or Greek-style yoghurt, full fat or fat-free to choice
1 teaspoon caster sugar
1 lemon, squeezed
1 teaspoon of coarsely ground black pepper
½ teaspoon of paprika
fresh chives, chopped

Fillet and **skin** the fish. (It will have been gutted and cleaned prior to smoking). Put most of the lemon juice, all the yoghurt, sugar and half of the fish into a large bowl. **Remove** any bones you can see and **blend** the mixture into a smooth paste using a fork or a hand blender.

Break the other half of the fish into chunks and **stir** them into the mixture with a fork, **adding** the black pepper as you stir, and again keeping an eye out for bones. This will produce a pâté-like consistency to which you can **add** a few chopped chives. Add more lemon juice as you wish.

Serve the pâté in ramekins, and top with a single black olive for decoration.

SMOKED MACKEREL WITH GOOSEBERRY SAUCE

People are often surprised to learn that gooseberries and mackerel go so well together. They go so well that the French word for gooseberry is *groseille à maquereau*, the oily fish and the low-sugared fruit making frequent partners.

I have found that well smoked mackerel with gooseberry sauce makes an excellent supper dish, the sweet yet sharp sauce complementing the fish admirably.

Ingredients (Serves 2)
1 good sized smoked mackerel

For the gooseberry sauce (to be prepared in advance):
250g green or amber gooseberries
100 ml water
10g of butter
30g of Demerara sugar (or more or less as you wish)
half a smallish lemon, squeezed

Prepare the fish by separating the two sides and cutting away poor quality belly flesh and bones. **Skin** each fillet, which is extremely easy as the skin slips straight off.

Prepare the sauce **well in advance** following the recipe on page 218.

Now **reheat** the gooseberry juice and **stir** in the sugar and the lemon juice to make the sauce. Let the sauce **simmer** for quite a while to let it reduce, thus concentrating its flavour. Allow the sauce to cool and refrigerate for a couple of hours before serving.

Sprats

PRAWNS WITH A PURÉE OF FLAGEOLET BEANS

This surprisingly delicious little dish – it really is especially good and makes a wonderful first course or even a very light lunch – is simplicity itself to prepare. I stumbled across the idea quite by chance when I wondered what to do with some prawns to make something a little different. Having some flageolet beans and knowing how attractive they are when made into a purée with olive oil and garlic I decided to match the purée with the prawns. The dish can equally well be made with canellini beans.

Ingredients (Serves 2)
150g of shelled prawns
250g of flageolet beans (1 tin ready cooked)
1 knob of butter
1 tablespoon of olive oil
2 cloves of garlic, crushed
½ lemon, squeezed

Drain the beans and wash them thoroughly (a standard sized tin will produce the correct weight of beans). Put them in a mixing bowl **adding** the butter, the olive oil, the crushed garlic and the lemon juice. **Mix roughly** with a fork and then, with a hand blender, **make the purée**, adding a little more olive oil if necessary to produce the consistency you like.

Now **add** the prawns to the purée, mix them in with a fork and **warm gently** on a very low heat. Serve on a lightly warmed plate.

BROWN SHRIMPS AND SAMPHIRE

I stumbled across this idea while perusing the fish counter at Maximus Sustainable Fishing near Aldeburgh. Being somewhat stuck for an interesting start to dinner that evening I looked at the wide variety of attractive fish on offer hoping to find some smoked prawns. I was thrown for a moment when told that they had sold out but then a bowl of deep green super-fresh marsh samphire caught my eye at the same moment as a bowl of peeled brown shrimps. That was it! A handful of shrimps, a little samphire mixed in, gently warmed in a saucepan with a knob of butter was the answer. And absolutely delicious it was!

Samphire is a perennial herb which grows in the wild on the salt marshes by the sea. Its season is short, and this dish is one for summer only. In early summer samphire is fresh and green, but by September dulls in colour and the plants tend to become a little woody.

Ingredients (Serves 2)
100g of North Atlantic brown shrimps, peeled
a handful of samphire
a knob of butter
a dash of lemon juice

Wash and dry the samphire well, because it is extremely salty. Trim it and discard the lower part of the stem and cut it into short-ish lengths.

Melt the knob of butter gently in a saucepan, **add** the samphire and turn it about so that it becomes well lubricated. Then **add** the shrimps and mix well. **Warm** the mix through over a low heat and then serve.

If you have any scallop shells they look rather attractive filled with the shrimps and samphire.

SHRIMPS WITH GHERKINS, CAPERS AND OLIVES

Like the shrimps and samphire, this charming little hors d'oeuvre was created quite spontaneously and I really rather enjoy it. One can, of course, omit any one of the vegetables if one prefers.

I think it is worthwhile to stick to gherkins of the sweet variety, as they chime nicely with the sweetness of the shrimps, and it is important, as always, to wash the capers very thoroughly indeed as they may have the unwelcome taste of the vinegar or salt in which they may have been stored. Olive stones are not welcome either, so be sure to check the olives carefully first.

This dish makes a good first course, but if the quantities are doubled it would do very well for a light lunch, perhaps accompanied by a chunk of pain de campagne and a small glass of dry white Bordeaux.

Ingredients (Serves 2)
150g of North Atlantic shrimps, peeled
1 tablespoon of sweet gherkins, finely diced
1 tablespoon of capers, washed thoroughly
1 tablespoon of black olives, pitted

Simply **combine** the ingredients in an open pan, **pour** on sufficient olive oil to lubricate them, and **warm them gently** over a low heat for a couple of minutes. Serve warm, but by no means hot.

PRESSED SKATE

This makes an unusual and delicious first course, succulent and filled with the taste of the sea. It is so delicious that a larger quantity for main course seems an attractive idea, and it makes a wonderful light lunch.

Ingredients (Serves 4)
1 large skate wing
olive oil
1 small tomato, very finely diced
2 small lemons, squeezed
1 small shallot, sliced
4 black olives
peppercorns

Make a **simple court bouillon**★ in a lidded pan using a sliced shallot, lemon juice and peppercorns.

To **poach** the fish bring the bouillon to the boil, **plunge** the skate wing into it, bring it back to the boil and then simmer gently for six to seven minutes according to size and thickness. Be sure to replace the lid.

Allow the fish to cool and then **scrape** off all the flesh and put it in a pudding basin. Dice, **very finely**, a small quantity of tomato and **add** it to the fish. **Add** the juice of one of the small lemons. **Mix** everything by hand using a fork **adding** a little olive oil.

Press the mixture gently into four ramekins and place one pitted black olive on top of each for decoration. Refrigerate.

★ *Court bouillon, p.132*

SKATE AND SPINACH SALAD

This is a very pleasing little first course which I referred to in 'Beginnings', being one of the first three recipes I wrote in my notebook having much enjoyed it at a restaurant in France. As the skate landed in Suffolk is always excellent – usually North Sea caught Thornback skate – the idea of matching a fish with a few spinach leaves is attractive for someone who is starting to cook as it needs nothing more than a poached skate and a pretty arrangement of foliage.

This dish makes an attractive light lunch, and no-one will realise how easy it is.

Ingredients (Serves 2)
1 good sized skate wing
baby spinach leaves
1 lime, halved
1 lemon, squeezed
2 black olives, pitted
light vinaigrette dressing

Make a **court bouillon**★ in a lidded pan using the ingredients of **your choice** from the court bouillon recipe. To **poach** the fish bring the bouillon to the boil, **plunge** the skate wing into it, bring it back to the boil and then leave the fish to simmer gently for six to seven minutes according to size and thickness. Be sure to replace the lid.

When cooked, **scrape** the flesh off the skate in lengths. Put them into a bowl together with some lemon juice. **Mix** the lemon juice well with the fish and let it all cool.

Season the spinach sparingly with a light vinaigrette of olive oil and white wine vinegar in the proportions three to one, and then lay the lengths of skate attractively on top of the spinach leaves. Place half a lime on each plate and decorate the top of each salad with one black olive.

★ *Court bouillon, p.132; Vinaigrette; p.56*

FISH MAIN COURSES

BRILL OR TURBOT, BAKED

Brill and turbot, the two most noble of all the flatfish, may both be cooked in the same way. They can be poached, grilled or baked. Poaching a whole turbot ideally requires a special turbot kettle on account of its size, and it is a safe bet that most households have scarcely heard of this mysterious apparatus, yet alone possess one. Grilling needs very close attention and much practice to take account of the thickness and temperature of the fish and the strength of the grill. Baking is less demanding for the cook, and produces a really lovely result, which is true not just for brill and turbot but for a wide variety of fish. These simple instructions work equally well for both brill and turbot.

> **Ingredients (Serves 2+)**
> 1 whole brill of around 800g (or 1 small whole turbot)
> a knob of butter
> 2 limes (or 1 lemon) for wedges and juice
> olive oil and herbs of Provence

For a whole fish: **Preheat** the oven to Gas 5, 190C.

Sparingly **oil** both sides of the fish using a pastry brush. **Place** a knob of butter on top. Lightly sprinkle with herbs. Bake for about 30 minutes.

If you ask the fishmonger to cut the fillets on one side partly free from the backbone, but without detaching them from the sides of the body – I call it butterflying – they will easily come away from the bone when cooked and look impressive on the plate. Serve with wedges of lime and a little lime juice.

For fillets: **Preheat** the oven to Gas 5, 190C.

Bake very simply. Lightly oil the fillets on each side and **wrap them loosely** in a parcel of baking paper, **skin side down**, with a knob of butter on top. Lightly sprinkle with herbs. **Bake** for about 25 minutes.

If a paper parcel is not used, lightly oil the fillets and bake **skin side up** for about 20 minutes. Sprinkle the herbs and place a knob of butter on top. Keep the fish moist with the juice of one lime, or a splash of white wine.

Wine suggestion: a distinguished white Burgundy such as Puligny-Montrachet.

COD BRANDADE (BRANDADE DE MORUE)

Cod brandade is one of the traditional dishes of Provence. It is based on salt cod. Having been salted and dehydrated the cod is then reconstituted by desalting. It is then poached. With skin and bones removed, the fish is then blended together with warm milk, olive oil and a little garlic to make a purée, and is served as a canapé, or as a first or main course. This simple dish is just so scrumptious, I adore it!

In the Marseille area, cod brandade contains potato which inevitably makes it into a meal by itself, but the recipe here is based on a simple method from rural Provence. As salt cod is not very readily available in Britain, a shortened version of salting and desalting is used, although I do not pretend that the result – whilst still most enjoyable – will be quite so memorable as what you might find on a Friday night in a simple country restaurant in the Luberon.

Ingredients (Serves 2)
350g of cod, first salted in sea salt, later desalted
3 cloves of garlic, crushed
2 tablespoons of full fat milk, with more for poaching
2 tablespoons of olive oil
Maldon salt and black pepper

First of all, lay the fish on a good bed of sea salt, and **cover** it with salt thickly. Leave it for 24 hours in the fridge. Then **remove** it from the salt, and **soak** it in **several changes** of fresh water all day to desalt it thoroughly.

To cook, **poach** the cod in a 50/50 mixture of milk and water. Poach by **simmering gently** for about 7 minutes. Remove the cod for skinning and de-boning. Gently warm the milk and the olive oil **separately**.

Place the cod in a saucepan with the crushed garlic and break it up thoroughly with a fork. **Stir in** the milk and olive oil separately to make a smooth creamy purée using a wooden spoon. Season and stir again. Lightly blend if you wish.

Wine suggestion: Bandol rosé.

Beach activities

COD LOIN WRAPPED IN PROSCIUTTO

A loin of pork is familiar to everyone, but a loin of cod may need explanation.

The loin, and the cheeks for which there is a separate First Course recipe, are the choice parts of the fish. The loin is the thick end of a filleted side, and for this dish it will be fashioned by the fishmonger into a skinless and boneless steak. The strip of fatty belly will be removed together with any skin or bone leaving a long steak. A good sized fish will yield a steak of about 350–400g which can be cut into two portions when cooked. For this recipe the whole steak is wrapped in prosciutto ham from Parma or San Daniele, prior to roasting. The whole operation is extremely simple to do and the result is delicious. I sometimes do this with hake, which is equally successful.

> **Ingredients (Serves 2)**
> 1 loin of cod of about 350–450g
> 3 thin slices of prosciutto
> herbs of Provence
> 2 medium sized tomatoes, halved
> thyme, dried

Preheat the oven to Gas 6, 200C.

Sprinkle a few Provençal herbs on top of the fish and **wrap** it in the ham and place it on a lightly oiled baking tray. Place a little crushed garlic on each half-tomato and then cover them with dried thyme.

Roast the fish and tomatoes for about 25–30 minutes. Serve with wedges of lemon or lime.

Wine suggestion: a light red or rosé from Anjou-Saumur in the Loire valley.

FAST FISH

I have called this recipe Fast Fish because it is the perfect example of how extremely quickly an excellent piece of fish can be cooked. It takes less time than is needed to cook an unhealthy burger and the fish will be thoroughly delicious. Fast Fish makes **the** perfect recipe for a beginner.

To cook fish this way simply involves the gentle use of hot lemon juice and olive oil to heat the fillet through, the steam producing a poaching effect which leaves the fish succulent and tasty. I might have called the recipe 'fillet of salmon sautéed in olive oil and lemon juice' or simply 'a quick lunch for one' but it is possible to use it for so many fish so I have left it just as Fast Fish. Here it is!

Ingredients (1 portion per person)
a portion (about 175g) of fresh salmon fillet or a fillet of plaice (or similar)
1 large lemon, squeezed
2 tablespoons of olive oil
herbs of Provence and garlic

Warm the oil and lemon juice in a lidded frying pan. **Place** the fillets **skin side down** in the pan, sprinkle lightly with dried herbs, and increase the heat. Use the lid to trap the steam. **Ensure** the skin does not stick to the pan by moving the fish with a spatula. If the portions are thickly cut turn them briefly on each side before turning them back on their skin to finish. Once the flesh has become opaque the fish will be cooked. To be certain, use the 'Is it Done?' test★.

If you wish to add anything, tomatoes and olives cook well with the fish.

Wine suggestion: for the beginner anything to celebrate success! Otherwise a cool Chablis or Petit Chablis will be perfect.

★ *'Is it Done?' test, p.84*

FINNAN HADDOCK AND POACHED EGG

Finnan haddock has been traditionally cold-smoked on green wood and peat in North East Scotland since the C17. This is in contrast to the perhaps more famous hot smoked haddock from Arbroath locally called Arbroath smokies. These can be bought by mail order. Smoked haddock has always been popular and is smoked all over Britain. You need to find a haddock which is lightly oak-smoked and, of course, undyed. Dyes used in fish are suspect from a health perspective and should be avoided.

This dish makes an excellent breakfast or light lunch.

Ingredients (Serves 2)
1 haddock fillet, lightly smoked, of about 300g
milk
a small knob of butter
2 eggs, poached

Bring to a simmer a wide lidded pan of cold water with a few black peppercorns and a bay leaf. Once that point has been reached **immerse** the fish, bring the water **back to a simmer** and turn off the heat completely. **Poach it skin side down** in the steaming liquid for six or seven minutes according to thickness. Keep the lid on. In a separate pan **poach** the eggs.

Shortly before the fish is ready make a light sauce. In a small saucepan **place** four tablespoons of the poaching water over a lively heat to reduce the water to concentrate the flavour. Then **melt** a knob of butter in another small pan and **add** a dessert spoon of the reduced poaching water and a dessert spoon of milk. **Stir** well together over a gentle heat.

Before the sauce starts to boil or froth, serve the fish skin side down with a poached egg on top together with a little of the sauce.

This is often served as a breakfast dish and is complemented by a good cup of Colombian coffee.

FISH PIE WITH LEMON MASHED POTATOES

Fish pie! What could be more British – British to the core – nourishing, warming, unsophisticated and comforting and well suited to British weather rather like a naval duffle coat. I hesitated before including this recipe because pleasing as fish pie undoubtedly is, it is rather more complicated and fiddly than the other recipes in this book although it is not inherently difficult. The true beginner will be able to achieve an excellent result with just a little help from a more experienced cook. No book aiming to introduce the reader to cooking could possibly be complete without a recipe for fish pie. It is a most enjoyable dish and will repay the cook, beginner or expert, handsomely in satisfaction.

It is important always to have good ingredients. So it is best to make up your own fish mix. A ready-made mix is often a collection of offcuts and pieces of belly fat and unlikely to be particularly good. To make your own, buy pieces of white fish, smoked and oily fish, and ready cooked shelled prawns. The ideal species are cod, hake, haddock, plaice, smoked haddock, fresh salmon and fresh Atlantic prawns. At least one smoked fish is important. The purists will argue about the inclusion of fresh salmon. I like it and always use it.

Ingredients (Serves 4)
500g of cod, haddock, smoked haddock, plaice, salmon and shelled Atlantic prawns
1 onion, well chopped
500 ml (approximately) of milk
400g (approximately) of potatoes after having been peeled
2 eggs, hard boiled
2 bay leaves
a few black peppercorns
For the sauce
50g of butter and 75g of white flour

The method is best followed step by step:

Preheat the oven to Gas 6, 200C.

Step 1   **Boil** 2 eggs, but not too hard. Eight minutes is ideal.

Step 2   **Prepare** the lemon mashed potatoes★.

Step 3   While the potatoes are cooking (if they are diced they will take about 15 minutes) almost **cover** the fish pieces with milk in a wide lidded pan. Do not include the prawns.

Step 4   **Add** the chopped onion, the bay leaves and a few peppercorns to the pan with the fish and place it on a gentle heat bringing it up to the boil. Just as boiling point is reached turn off the heat and leave it for six minutes with the lid on.

Step 5   **Remove** the fish and drain the remainder through a sieve. Keep the milk for use in Step 7. **Discard** the onion, bay and peppercorns. Put the fish skin-side up on a chopping board. Carefully **remove** the skins and break the fish into flaky lumps with a fork. Put the fish to one side, and add the prawns to it.

Step 6   Now **prepare** the sauce. In a large saucepan melt the butter gently and add the flour. **Stir** it all in well and keep stirring for a further minute or two. It will become a little gritty, but keep stirring to get rid of any lumps. Then **remove** from the heat.

Step 7   **Add** the milk (already saved at Step 5) to the sauce extremely slowly, stirring after each addition of milk. A hand whisk may help to get rid of any lumps. Keep stirring until you have a smooth milk sauce.

Step 8   To create the final fish sauce, simply **stir** all the fish and prawns into the milk sauce.

Step 9   **Cut** the two eggs lengthways and put them in an ovenproof dish, and **pour** the final fish sauce, that is to say all the milk and fish together, over them. Then spread the lemon mashed potatoes evenly on top.

Final step   **Bake** the finished pie in the oven for 30 minutes.

Wine suggestion: Sauvignon blanc.

★ *Lemon mashed potatoes, p.195*

HADDOCK FILLET WITH ANCHOVY SAUCE

Haddock is a satisfying, meaty white fish yet one that can be a bit dull if not dressed up a little. I always feel that it could be so good if it were to play a more imaginative role than being consumed with chips and vinegar out of a copy of the Yorkshire Post or the East Anglian Daily Times in the time hallowed British seaside manner. Nor do I mean just throwing in some prawns with it. It needs a sauce, and with the right one it can be delicious. For me, anchovy sauce more than does the trick, quite powerful and brimming with character.

Ingredients (Serves 2)
350–375g of haddock fillet
1 lemon, sliced
anchovy sauce*

Preheat the oven to Gas 5, 190C

Place the fillet in a roasting dish on a bed of sliced lemon, having brushed the fish very lightly with olive oil on both sides. Place the fish **skin side up** and **bake** for about 20 minutes.

While the fish is baking **prepare** the anchovy sauce*, ensuring that it is hot when it is poured over the fish. Serve the fish **skin side down**.

A scrumptious accompaniment for the fish is lemon potato* together with Provençal tomatoes* which add a splash of colour on the plate.

Wine suggestion: the rosés from the Côtes-de-Provence chime well with the aromas from powerful fish, albeit surprisingly.

---

* *Anchovy sauce, p.206; Lemon mashed potatoes, p.195; Tomatoes à la Provençale, p.202*

SMOKED HADDOCK WITH SPICED CORIANDER LENTILS

This 'guest recipe' has been very kindly contributed by Peter Harrison, the highly regarded and well-known independent Suffolk chef.

Peter started his cooking career at Annecy in the Haute Savoie, and now runs his own independent catering business. He takes special pride in seeking out the best possible raw ingredients making the utmost good use of the seasons and all that the Suffolk countryside can provide, both cultivated and wild. Amongst his specialities are venison, partridge, mutton and locally smoked haddock and it is his recipe for smoked haddock with spiced coriander lentils that I am very delighted to include in this book.

Ingredients (Serves 4)

4 fillets of smoked haddock, each of 150–200g, skinned and pin-boned
250g of Puy lentils (dried not tinned)
1 thumb of ginger, peeled and sliced
1 small red chilli, chopped
4 cloves of garlic, peeled
6 medium shallots, peeled and sliced
300ml white wine
100ml of cyder (Aspall's Suffolk cyder if available)
200ml of Greek-style full fat yoghurt (Marybelle if available)
2 large bunches of coriander
seasoning

Preheat the oven to Gas 6, 200C.

Rinse the lentils under cold water. Place them in a saucepan and cover them with double the volume of water as lentils. Do not add salt as this will hamper the cooking process. Bring up to a **simmer** and **cook until tender** which will take approximately 15–20 minutes. Turn off, drain and put them back in the saucepan.

In a **separate saucepan** place **all the other ingredients apart from** the coriander and yoghurt. Bring to the boil and **simmer** for 8–10 minutes. **Add** the yoghurt, bring back to a **simmer** and cook for a **further** 5 minutes. **Add** the coriander and **blend** until smooth. **Season**.

Add the sauce to the pan containing the lentils, and **warm gently**.

Bake the haddock for about 6–10 minutes depending on your oven, or until cooked. **Make a bed** of the lentil sauce and place the haddock **on top**.

Dress with a coriander sprig.

Wine suggestion: a dry Riesling from Alsace.

HAKE PROVENÇAL

Whenever I make this dish I never fail to enthuse about the wonderful qualities of hake. It is just so juicy and delicious that it is a matter of amazement that it is not more popular in Britain whereas the French, and particularly the Spaniards, buy it in huge quantities. This simple recipe which is nothing more than hake baked under a sauce made from onions, tomatoes, olives and garlic creates an attractive dish in the Provençal manner.

Ingredients (Serves 2)
350–400g of hake loin, skinned and divided into two
150g of white onions, finely chopped
225–250g of tomatoes after having been peeled, de-seeded and chopped
3 garlic cloves, crushed
a handful of black olives, pitted and chopped
olive oil

Preheat the oven to Gas 5, 190C.

Skin the fish, or preferably ask your fishmonger to do it as hake is delicate and tricky to skin without tearing the fillet. **Chop** the onions as finely as you possibly can and **peel, de-seed and chop** the tomatoes.

Cover the base of a lidded saucepan with olive oil and very **gently cook** the onions, together with the crushed garlic, until they have softened and discoloured. Now **add** the chopped tomatoes and chopped olives, stir well, and replace the lid of the saucepan and **simmer**, stirring from time to time.

Put the hake (a good thick fillet) in a small, lightly oiled baking tray, preferably just large enough to accommodate it. Once the sauce has fully softened and thickened, use all of it to cover the fish **quite thickly**.

Envelop the baking tray with baking paper and **bake** for 45 minutes.

Wine suggestion: Sancerre.

HALIBUT BAKED IN BREADCRUMBS WITH PROVENÇAL TOMATOES

For this dish a good piece of wild halibut fillet is needed rather than a halibut steak. A meaty and moist fillet baked very simply with a covering of white breadcrumbs is delicious, and when accompanied by Provençal tomatoes, creamed potatoes and a green vegetable such as broccoli, creates a lovely dish, easily prepared and cooked. Note that wild halibut is very much under threat.

This recipe works admirably for hake, too.

Ingredients (Serves 2)
fillet of wild halibut, about 375g
1 egg
white breadcrumbs
2 large tomatoes
garlic
olive oil
black pepper

Preheat the oven to Gas 5, 190C.

Wash the fish and dry with kitchen roll. Prepare the Provençal tomatoes* and place them in the oven 15 minutes before the halibut. Both fish and tomatoes will therefore be ready at the same time.

To **prepare** the fish, first break the egg on to a dinner plate and mix the yolk and white together with a fork. **Make** the breadcrumbs from not-too-fresh white bread using a hand held blender and **cover** a second dinner plate with the crumbs.

Now **dip** both sides of the fish in the egg before **dipping** the egged fish in the breadcrumbs. **Place** the fish in a baking tray and season with black pepper.

Bake for about 17–20 minutes in the oven (the tomatoes are already baking of course) keeping the temperature at Gas 5, 190C.

Wine suggestion: a dry rosé from Provence such as Bandol.

---

* *Tomatoes à la Provençale, p.202*

GRILLED YARMOUTH HERRINGS WITH A MUSTARD SAUCE

I find it rather charming to call them Yarmouth herrings, although people do not bother to give them their full title nowadays. The name is a relic from the days of Queen Victoria when most herrings were landed at Great Yarmouth on the Norfolk-Suffolk border. Yarmouth was the epicentre of a massive herring fishery and in the early C20 the prosperity of the town grew on the activities of the drifter fleet based there. Nowadays, herrings in relatively small numbers are landed in many fishing towns and villages on the East coast of Britain.

Available for most of the year but at their best in the Autumn, herrings make a wonderful Omega-3 packed meal on their own. This simple recipe brings that little extra something to the humble herring by adding the tang of the mustard fields of Norfolk. For total authenticity and the best result use Colman's mustard from the yellow tin.

Ingredients (Serves 2)
2 good sized herrings, gutted and cleaned
a good dollop of butter, softened
Colman's English mustard made up according to instructions
a few drops of lemon juice and olive oil

The quantities in this recipe are necessarily imprecise. The size of herrings is extremely variable, and the strength of mustard, especially English mustard, is equally so. The sauce must therefore be made to the taste of those who eat it.

For the sauce, **make up** the mustard as a paste to the strength you like in accordance with the written instructions on the tin. Then soften a knob of butter in a small saucepan and stir in an appropriate amount of mustard to produce a soft, creamy mixture. Then **stir in** a few drops of olive oil and a very little lemon juice.

Brush the herrings with olive oil and grill them for three to four minutes on each side, blistering but not burning the skins. Serve with the sauce on the side.

Wine suggestion: no wine – Adnams Southwold bitter.

JOHN DORY BAKED WHOLE

John Dory comes high up the batting order for ugliness, although it is not in the monkfish league which is in a class of its own. John Dory is easily recognisable on the fishmonger's slab; it is an oval, thin, silvery bronze fish sporting rather vicious fins, but its notable feature is a large black spot on each side which is said to be St. Peter's thumbprint. Its French name is in fact St. Pierre. It has the most delicately tasting flesh which requires simple treatment in the kitchen despite the complicated recipes that are to be found in many cookery books. To bake a John Dory whole is easy and satisfying. Ask the fishmonger to remove the head and fins, and it will be ready for baking. Lightly brush it with olive oil and garnish it with a knob of butter, herbs of Provence and a little black pepper. It is admirably complemented by mashed potatoes, aubergines and an anchovy sauce★.

Remember that a John Dory yields no more than 40% of its weight in edible fillet.

Ingredients (Serves 2)
2 whole John Dory, about 450g each
butter
herbs of Provence
black pepper
1 lemon, wedged; or 1 lime, halved

Preheat the oven to Gas 5, 190C.

Brush both sides of each fish with olive oil and **sprinkle** lightly with pepper and herbs of Provence. Place a knob of butter on each fish and **wrap** them in a single **loose parcel** of baking paper.

Bake for about 20 minutes. Fillet when cooked and serve the portions on the plates with a wedge of lemon or half a lime.

Wine suggestion: a Pouilly-fumé from the Loire.

★ *Anchovy sauce, p.206*

The fish market

MACKEREL PROVENÇAL

This is the most wonderful way to eat mackerel, a fish which has your cardiovascular system in ecstasy, marvelling at the shot of nutrients it is enjoying at one sitting! Health benefits aside, mackerel is a beautiful, sleek, muscular and delicious fish, and has the added attraction of being widely available for most of the year and at remarkably low prices. Mackerel is often thought to be rather fatty, but cooked in the Provençal manner it will prove to be one of the favourites around your table.

Ingredients (Serves 2)
2 mackerel
1 medium sized onion, finely chopped
2 good sized tomatoes, finely chopped
4 garlic cloves, crushed
1 glass of dry white wine
1 heaped teaspoon of dried thyme, and 2 good sprigs of fresh parsley

Preheat the oven to Gas 7, 220C.

Clean and wash the fish, remove the heads and place the fish in a roasting tray.

Peel the tomatoes. **Chop** the onion finely, **crush** the garlic and **dice** the peeled tomatoes and **fry** them together gently in olive oil to make a sauce.

Once the onion, garlic and tomato has nicely softened (this will take around 10 minutes) **pour** the dry white wine over the fish and then surround them with the tomato sauce.

Bake for 15 minutes. Sprinkle with chopped parsley on serving.

Wine suggestion: a dry white such as a Viognier from South West France.

MONKFISH, SHALLOTS AND TOMATOES IN A WHITE WINE SAUCE

Once given to the cat but now cooked for kings, monkfish enjoys an important place on the very best tables. During the late C20 it was realised by chefs that the texture and taste of monkfish is not so very dissimilar from lobster and could be turned into a delicious dish and sold at a premium price. Simple to cook, it can give great pleasure. Fillets need to be de-membraned to ensure that the fish does not contort in the cooking, but a good fishmonger will prepare it as necessary. It is also much better when cooked in the form of small steaks rather than the fillet being cooked whole which can produce a somewhat rubbery consistency. This particular recipe is delicious.

Ingredients (Serves 2)
1 monkfish tail of about 375g, filleted and cut into small steaks
2 shallots (torpedo shape) very finely chopped
3 medium sized tomatoes, chopped
a good knob of butter
1 glass of dry white wine
a few sprigs of parsley, chopped

Spread out the finely chopped shallots in a saucepan, just **cover** them with an inexpensive dry white wine such as Muscadet (or dry Aspall's Suffolk cyder) and **soak** them for about an hour.

Slice each fillet into diagonal steaks about 2cm thick. **Melt** a good-sized knob of butter in a wide covered pan, **add** the shallots and cook them gently for a few minutes. Then **add** the chopped tomatoes and parsley to the shallots, **mix** them all together thoroughly and increase the heat a little. **Cook** for three or four minutes.

Now **turn up** the heat to a moderate level, **place the fish on top** of the shallots and tomatoes, replace the lid on the pan and **cook** for eight minutes.

Serve with a white wine sauce★ following the recipe in this book.

Wine suggestion: a characterful wine with a blend of fruit and acidity such as an Alsatian Sylvaner. Vintage Pol Roger champagne would be wonderful.

★ White wine sauce, p.213

RED MULLET WITH A GARNISH OF TAPENADE

There is something rather special about the pinky brown, red mullet. Not only does it have that unique and appealing rosy blush which so attracted the Roman bourgeoisie two thousand years ago, but it has its own unique and very particular flavour which goes so well with Mediterranean salads. It is especially good with black olives or tomatoes. When garnished with black olive tapenade★ or tomato tapenade★ it is one of those many dishes that takes your mind immediately to the sea and sunshine of the Mediterranean.

It is a fish which needs to be really fresh. It should be firm to the touch when purchased and eaten the same day or the day after to be at its best. It will cook under the grill admirably, and this simple recipe (for a whole fish) just requires the belly cavity to be filled with a couple of fresh rosemary sprigs, the skin moistened all over with olive oil and the grilling to be limited to four to five minutes on each side. It can, of course, be filleted and then grilled skin uppermost. This is perhaps a better method for those who are less adept at surgery as this fish is rather bony.

Ingredients (Serves 2)
2 fresh red mullets, cleaned and gutted
fresh rosemary sprigs
olive oil
black olive tapenade★; or
tomato tapenade★

Preheat the grill. **Prepare** the tapenade following the recipe★. **Ensure** the fish has been **properly cleaned, washed and dried** and **fill** the belly cavity with fresh rosemary sprigs. **Moisten** the skin on both sides lightly with olive oil using a pastry brush and place under a medium to high grill for 4–5 minutes a side.

Fillet the fish, and serve on a light bed of tapenade. (If grilling fillets, grill them for about 5 minutes with the skin uppermost). Serve with a rocket salad.

Wine suggestion: not easy! try a generic Pinot Noir from Burgundy.

★ *Black olive tapenade, p.27; Tomato tapenade, p.30*

ROAST FILLET OF PLAICE ON A BED OF ROSEMARY POTATOES

To cook plaice on a bed of rosemary potatoes with tomatoes and olives is most gratifying. This Mediterranean idea complements the fish beautifully and is successful for a variety of flat white fish, whether filleted or on the bone, but the cooking times will naturally vary.

Ingredients (Serves 2)
2 plaice fillets
4 good sized potatoes, sliced
14 cherry tomatoes
12 black olives
4 sprigs of fresh rosemary
6 garlic cloves, crushed
olive oil

Preheat the oven to Gas 7, 220C.

Step 1: **Peel** the potatoes and **slice** them to about 5mm thick. **Boil** them until they are virtually soft enough to eat. Let them dry. Then **spread** them out with the rosemary sprigs and crushed garlic, in a roasting tray wide enough to take the fillets side by side. **Lubricate** generously with olive oil and season. **Roast** the potatoes for 15–20 minutes so that they start to brown.

Step 2: **Lay** the fillets of plaice on the bed of potatoes **skin side up**, and brush lightly with olive oil. **Add** the tomatoes and the olives. **Return** the tray to the oven and **roast** the ensemble for about 15 minutes according to weight and size (a whole plaice will need about 20 minutes).

Wine suggestion: a modest dry white such as Entre-deux-mers.

BAKED FILLET OF PLAICE WITH SUNBLUSH TOMATOES AND OLIVES

It cannot be claimed that this is a Provençal dish since plaice is not particularly common in the Mediterranean. However, the plaice found in British waters is quite delicious and this fish happily marries with a little Mediterranean influence. It is quick and easy to prepare and also quick to cook. Avoid plaice in the Spring which is its spawning period and make this a summer or Autumn dish.

Ingredients (Serves 2)
2 good sized plaice fillets
150g of sunblush tomatoes
50g of black olives, pitted and halved
2 handfuls of white breadcrumbs
olive oil

Preheat the oven to Gas 6, 200C.

Wash and dry the fillets. **Oil** both sides lightly, using a pastry brush. **Lay** them on a baking tray, ideally an oval oven-proof porcelain dish, with the **skin-side down** and ensuring they are lying flat. **Spread** the tomatoes and olives evenly on top and then **sprinkle** a handful of breadcrumbs over the fish.

Pour two tablespoons of olive oil into the tray so that the oil surrounds the fish.

Bake for about 16–18 minutes according to the weight and size of the fish.

Wine suggestion: a modest country rosé such as one from Corbieres or Provence.

SALMON FUSILLI

This is a wonderful supper dish – quick and easy to prepare, nutritious and satisfying – a favourite. The salmon, flavoured with the anchovy, and mixed with one of the best pasta products is scrumptious. It is well worthwhile buying the best wholemeal fusilli you can find.

Ingredients (Serves 2)
350g of fresh fillet of salmon
1 x 30g tin of anchovies in olive oil
175g (approx.) of wholemeal fusilli
1 heaped tablespoon of tomato purée
a little fresh parsley, chopped

Warm the salmon in the microwave for about three minutes at medium intensity. The salmon needs to be very lightly cooked, but cooked sufficiently for you to be able to peel the skin away quite easily.

Peel away and **discard** the skin. **Break** the fish into smallish pieces and put it in a heavy saucepan. **Cut** up the anchovies and **add** to the salmon. Now **add** the tomato purée and **mix** well together. Place the saucepan over a very gentle heat.

Boil the fusilli in vigorously boiling water according to the written instructions. While the fusilli is cooking stir the salmon mixture over the gentle heat. This will be sufficient to finish cooking the fish.

When the fusilli is ready, **remove** it from the heat, **drain**, and **serve** it on well warmed plates (pasta loses heat quickly), and complete the serving by putting the salmon mixture on top. **Sprinkle** with a little chopped parsley.

Wine suggestion: Bourgogne aligoté (often called the Muscadet of Burgundy) or Muscadet, if you prefer.

SARDINES À LA PROVENÇALE

Refreshing, nourishing and intense, sardines are better still with a glass of cool dry rosé from Provence. Grilled sardines get pretty close to escapism – holidays, sunshine, delicious food and wine. However, the recipe here is a true Provençal method which can easily be achieved with good fish which is occasionally caught off the South West coast of England or even very occasionally in the North Sea. Sardines à la Provençale are prepared in conjunction with the traditional flavours of Provence – olive oil, tomatoes, garlic, thyme and bay – all of which go so well with the inimitable taste and savour of fresh sardines and the sea.

Ingredients (Serves 2)
3 fresh sardines per person
1 lemon, halved
2 tomatoes, halved
crinkly parsley
2 good sprigs of fresh rosemary
herbs of Provence

Prepare the sardines: remove the heads and slit them open along the belly. Remove all the guts and **wash** under a cold tap and then roughly dry. Fill the belly cavity with sprigs of fresh rosemary. Place the sardines on the grill pan, **brush** them on both sides with olive oil and **sprinkle** them with herbs. **Halve** the tomatoes and season them with a pinch of dried herbs and place them with the fish ready for grilling.

Grill the fish for around four minutes on each side. At the same time grill the halved tomatoes. Once the skin of the fish begins to **bubble and brown** the sardines will be cooked.

Before serving drizzle the fish with a little olive oil and **sprinkle** them with freshly chopped parsley. **Add** two tomato halves to each serving, and squeeze half a lemon over each fish.

Wine suggestion: a Coteaux-varois-en-Provence rosé, from the Var.

WILD SEA BASS (OR BREAM) WHOLE ON THE BONE, BAKED

Wild sea bass releases all its lovely flavours when baked whole on the bone. The method of cooking is very straightforward. The main concern is to ensure that it does not overcook so that it retains its moistness and savours. The precise cooking time is difficult to lay down with any certainty. Much depends on the characteristics of the particular oven and the size and weight of the fish. However, this recipe will provide a workable guide for a sea bass or bream providing generous portions for two. A sea bass will yield 40–45% of its weight edible fillet. A bream is similar.

Preheat the oven to Gas 5, 190C.

For a fish of about 700g, **brush** it all over with olive oil and lay it in a roasting tray on a **bed of lemon** or lime slices. Cut four garlic cloves into **sharp shapes** and **pierce** the flesh with a sharp pointed knife and push in the cloves. Put one whole clove with a good sprig of thyme or rosemary into the belly cavity.

Bake uncovered for about 30 minutes. Always apply the 'Is it Done?' test. Serve with lime wedges. Bream is especially good with curly kale.

FILLETS, BAKED

When fillets are preferred rather than the whole fish this recipe provides a very appealing alternative. It saves the cook the surgical operation required for producing elegant portions from the whole fish once it is cooked, and has the benefit of combining delicate citrus flavours with the fish.

Preheat the oven to Gas 5, 190C.

Brush the base of the roasting tray with olive oil and **make a bed** of thin slices of **orange and lemon** on which to lay the fillets **skin side up**. Lightly brush the skin with garlic olive oil. Put a few sprigs of thyme or rosemary on top together with a light sprinkling of Provençal herbs. **Bake uncovered** for about 18 minutes.

Wine suggestion: Muscadet.

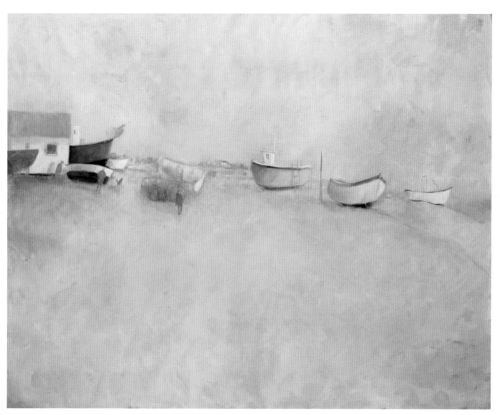

Aldeburgh fishing boats

BLACK BREAM WITH ONIONS AND GARLIC

Of the endless recipes for fish, the vast majority are simply garnishes, sauces and accompaniments. Supposedly they make the fish more interesting. Many of them of course do. But many more are unnecessary complications and probably bring little more pleasure but a great deal of work. A particular example is sole, for which there are hundreds of recipes. Consider Sole Duse: sole, filleted, stuffed, folded, poached, dressed in a savarin mould lined with risotto, dished and coated with Mornay sauce, set to gratin. Centre garnished with a salpicon (diced) of shrimps cohered with white wine sauce, sprinkled with chopped truffles! Undoubtedly delicious!

So abandon the idea of a stuffed sole! Try a simple, up-to-date dish like wild black bream with onions and garlic! You will not be disappointed!

Ingredients (Serves 2)
1 black bream, whole, of about 600g
1 large white onion, thinly sliced
plenty of garlic, chopped
½ a lemon, squeezed

Preheat the oven to Gas 5, 190C.

Slice the onion very thinly, and sauté lightly in olive oil together with at least six chopped garlic cloves for three to four minutes. **Spread** out most of it in an ovenproof fish dish. Put the rest in the belly of the fish. **Splash** the fish with olive oil and place it on top of the onion and garlic in the dish. **Add** a very little water to the dish.

Bake for 25–30 minutes turning the fish over after the first 10 minutes and serve with the lemon juice and parsley.

This may not get you three Michelin stars, but it will still be delicious. You will be pleased as will whoever accompanies you.

Wine suggestion: a dry white from the Dordogne such as Bergerac-sec.

WILD SEA TROUT POACHED WHOLE

A poached wild sea trout is really the high point of this book. Yet it is one of the easiest recipes to achieve. It will seem to be light years away from the very simple dishes you started with. A sea trout, or salmon trout, is a lovely fish and it is a matter of huge encouragement to know that it can be cooked to perfection just by applying a little love and care.

You do need, however, to buy a fish kettle. A fish kettle is a very simple piece of kitchen equipment which you might not have come across. It is a truly exciting moment going to buy one. I am not sure I had ever seen one until it was taken off the top shelf in the shop – one of those shops where the shelf nearest the ceiling secretes a fish kettle or two wrapped up in dusty brown paper. But to poach a good sized sea trout you have to have one and it is the passport to eating a really wonderful fish.

Ingredients (Serves 4–5)
1 whole sea trout of 1.5–1.7kg (this fish is caught under licence)
Court bouillon★

This method is ideal for a fish of a kilo or more, and will cook it very quickly. About 14–16 minutes should be enough, depending upon the actual weight of the fish. Ask the fishmonger to clean the fish but leave the head and tail.

First, **prepare** a court bouillon★ in the fish kettle following the instructions in this book. Make only so much as will **barely cover** the fish. A good court bouillon is the key to poaching any fish well. Its aromatic qualities enhance the flavours of the fish and it can be made in accordance with your own whims and fancies.

Once the court bouillon is ready place the fish gently in the boiling liquid so that it **barely covers the fish**, adding boiling water if insufficient. **Place over a low heat**, ideally over a ring or hotplate at each end of the kettle, but **do not allow** the bouillon to boil and bubble. It should do no more than **shimmer and shake**. After about 12 minutes apply the 'Is it Done?' test★.

When done, and the magnificent fish is presented whole to the assembled company, give yourself a pat on the back. Your guests certainly will.

Wine suggestion: a good quality Sancerre or Chablis.

★ *Court bouillon, p.132; 'Is it Done?' test, p.84*

SCALLOPS WITH CHORIZO ON A BED OF LEMON POTATOES

This provides a lovely combination of tastes. It is simple and quick to do. However, do take care when buying the scallops. Make sure that they have been harvested by divers and not trawled and, as for all bivalves, ensure that they are absolutely fresh. When it comes to the chorizo be equally vigilant. Ask your butcher if it contains anything other than pork. If it does, give it a miss. Traditional Spanish chorizo can contain products from animals you might well not want to eat! Don't be put off! Scallops with chorizo are delicious.

If you cannot find good chorizo sausage, but you do have some nice scallops, simply fry them gently in butter and serve them with lemon potatoes★.

> **Ingredients (Serves 2)**
> 12 scallops (Coquilles St. Jacques) harvested responsibly by divers
> small quantity of chorizo, diced
> olive oil
> 3 limes, squeezed (or one medium lemon)
> black pepper

Step 1: dice the chorizo and **dry fry** it in a pre-heated heavy pan for about 3 minutes. Set the chorizo to one side as soon as it has browned a little and released its fat, which will be voluminous. **Discard** the fat. Then **fry** the scallops in the same pan for a couple of minutes.

Step 2: now **combine** the chorizo with the scallops, **adding** most of the lime juice. **Fry** over a medium heat until the scallops have lightly browned by which time the chorizo will be cooked.

Serve with a light sprinkling of black pepper and the remaining drops of lime juice.

Wine suggestion: for the scallops and chorizo, no wine. For the scallops alone, non-vintage champagne or Sauvignon blanc.

★ *Lemon mashed potatoes, p.195*

SKATE WITH MASHED POTATO AND CAPER SAUCE

Always buy skate from a first class fishmonger. Beware of skate which smells faintly of ammonia and do not buy anything which has a strong smell. After the fish has been caught the natural urea in its body breaks down after a while (in common with sharks and other rays) into ammonia, and so an ammoniac fish is not fresh by definition. A good fishmonger will sell skate which is ready to eat.

Poaching is a satisfactory method of cooking skate so long as the poaching water is well prepared so as to make a simple court bouillon★. I also like pan frying in a little olive oil and lemon juice. Either method will be complemented by a simple caper sauce.

Ingredients (Serves 2)
1 good sized skate wing of around 700g
a good knob of butter
1 tablespoon of capers, well rinsed
1 lemon, squeezed
olive oil

Boil the potatoes until soft and prepare the fish in the meantime.

To poach, **prepare** a simple **court bouillon★** of lemon, shallots, peppercorns and bay. Bring the court bouillon to the boil in a large flat-bottomed pan and then **immerse** the fish and poach in the **gently simmering** liquid for around 6–7 minutes depending on size. Don't overcook it! It will be ready when the flesh easily scrapes away from the bone.

To pan-fry, lightly cover the base of the pan with olive oil and add the juice of the lemon. Fry gently until the fish has cooked through.

For the sauce: **wash** the capers very thoroughly. **Melt** a good knob of butter in a saucepan, season, and mix in the capers and lemon juice. **Mash** the potatoes with a little warmed milk (and lemon juice if you wish) and serve.

Wine suggestion: a crisp French white such as Sancerre.

★ *Court bouillon, p.132*

SOLE GRATIN

Whilst generally sticking to the rule of 'keep it simple' for delicate white fish, it is worthwhile plunging into deeper waters once confidence has been gained. The plethora of recipes for sole, both Lemon and Dover, is one of those excesses of the cookery world which I have mentioned elsewhere, but the following rather charming recipe is very appealing and well worth trying.

Ingredients (Serves 2)
4 sole fillets, Lemon or Dover
50g of butter
4 tablespoons of shallots, chopped
6 tablespoons of fish stock
6 tablespoons of white wine; or 3 tablespoons of cognac
breadcrumbs to cover
2 tablespoons of crinkly parsley, chopped

Preheat the oven to Gas 7, 220C.

Butter a fish dish (preferably oval ovenproof porcelain fish dish) and **sprinkle** the base with half the chopped parsley and shallots. **Season** and place the fish on top, **skin side down**. Now cover the fish with the rest of the chopped ingredients and top with breadcrumbs.

Add the white wine, or cognac, and the fish stock. Leave four knobs of butter on the fillets.

Bake for about 15 minutes. By this time the gratin should be beginning to brown very slightly. If it has not done so pass it under a hot grill **very quickly, but do not linger** or it will spoil. Apply the 'Is it Done?' test★.

Wine suggestion: a dry, fruity Alsatian Riesling.

★ *'Is it Done?' test, p.84*

DOVER SOLE WHOLE ON THE BONE, GRILLED (OR BAKED); FILLETS, BAKED

Grilled whole Dover sole on the bone is one of those English traditions which no self respecting London club or restaurant with any pretensions could possibly not offer, for it has been the staple food of businessmen and their guests for generations. The key to successful grilling is to judge the cooking time in accordance with the power of the grill and the weight and thickness of the fish. It is not difficult so long as one's attention is not distracted.

In contrast, however, fillets of Dover sole ideally lend themselves to being baked in the oven. The instructions here are extremely simple, and the huge number of complicated recipes created for sole over the last 150 years may happily be put on one side for another day or just left to the professionals.

To grill or bake whole Dover sole on the bone to serve 2 (a fish of about 750–800g or two smaller fish):

Preheat the grill to high. **Brush** the fish all over with melted butter before grilling and **be prepared** to add more. **Grill** for 4–5 minutes a side depending on the thickness of the fish. The butter will help to keep the fish moist but will eventually turn golden which is good, but **do not** let the butter burn. Serve with segments of lime.

To bake a whole Dover sole on the bone: **preheat** the oven to Gas 6, 200C.

Bake for about 20–25 minutes. If the skin has been removed from one side, bake with the **skin side up**. Lightly oil the tray. Place knobs of butter on the fish. If baking two smaller fish the cooking time will be shorter.

To **bake** fillets of a Dover sole: **preheat** the oven to Gas 6, 200C.

Fillets may be baked in 8–10 minutes depending on size, using a lightly oiled baking tray. If one side has been skinned, bake with the **skin sides up**. **Sprinkle** the fillets with mixed Provençal herbs or preferably with chopped fresh herbs. **Top** with a knob of butter and **splash** some white wine or dry cyder around the fish. This preserves the moisture in the fish while cooking.

Wine suggestion: a dry white Bordeaux or possibly an Alsatian Riesling.

LEMON SOLE, WHOLE ON THE BONE AND FILLETS, BAKED

Lemon sole may be baked very simply, either filleted or as a whole fish.

One of the great merits of this lovely fish is that it really needs nothing more with it than a knob of butter to bring out its delicate flavours, yet it has also been very well suited to the culinary imagination of the great chefs over the years. You will find simple but excellent recipes in this book, and sticking to these easy formulae will prove to be a splendid way to enjoy it.

Whether the sole is filleted or whole, I favour making a bed of sliced lemon on which to lay the fish in a baking tray.

Baked whole lemon sole on the bone:

Preheat the oven to Gas 6, 200C.

Brush over both sides with olive oil, and lay the fish on a bed of **lemon slices**. Scatter a few herbs of Provence over the fish and place a **knob of butter** on top.

Bake for 25–30 minutes for a fish of about 700g, large enough for two.

Baked fillets of lemon sole:

Preheat the oven to Gas 5, 190C.

Brush the fillets lightly with olive oil and lay them **skin side up** on a bed of **lemon slices**. **Scatter** a few Provençal herbs over the skins and place a **knob of butter** on top.

Bake uncovered for about 15 minutes depending on thickness and weight.

Wine suggestion: Chablis

LEMON SOLE FILLETS IN A FOIL PARCEL

This is a very lovely Provençal way of cooking fillets of lemon sole. The fish is quite delicate, and will retain a marvellous succulence and an exquisite taste with its garnish, and yet the recipe is extremely simple to do. In fact, it is perhaps a surprise that such an uncomplicated recipe can produce such a delicious result.

Ingredients (Serves 2)
2 fillets of lemon sole
1 lime, wedged
1 tomato, sliced
1 small onion, finely chopped
2 tablespoons of olive oil
seasoning

Preheat the oven to Gas 6, 200C.

Wash and dry the fillets. Place each fillet **skin side down** on a sheet of silver foil of a sufficient size to fold over the fish to make a loose parcel.

Chop the onion and **fry** the pieces extremely gently in butter so that they discolour but do not brown.

On top of each fillet **place** two slices of lime, two slices of tomato and a teaspoon or two of fried onion. **Season** with a little salt and black pepper.

Ensuring that the parcels will hold a liquid, **pour** a dessertspoon of olive oil over each fillet and wrap the foil loosely over the top to finish the parcel.

Place the parcels in a baking tray and **bake** for 20 minutes. Serve with lime wedges. Sauté potatoes in oil and garlic go well with this dish.

Wine suggestion: a fairly sharp dry wine such as Muscadet.

COURT BOUILLON

The need for a flavoured poaching liquid is extremely important for the enjoyment of any poached fish. A court bouillon is an aromatic stock in which fish is cooked. Simple to make up, a court bouillon can contain whichever herbs, spices and flavours that appeal to you.

The following are suggested ideas rather than recipes. They are ideas which seem to work well and will offer, at the least, some guidance. Fish which immediately come to mind as benefitting from a good court bouillon are skate, salmon and sea trout. I suggest using the first idea, without wine, for skate; and the second, with wine, for salmon and sea trout.

Court bouillon without wine:

water, sufficient to cover the fish in the pan
lemon juice and lemon zest
1 small carrot, sliced finely
a few black pepper corns, whole
1 white onion, finely chopped
bay leaf
1 tablespoon of red wine vinegar

Court bouillon with 2 glasses of white wine or dry cyder:

As above deleting the vinegar and adding:
fennel
garlic
fresh thyme, if available, otherwise dried

Simmer both these aromatic mixtures for 15 minutes prior to poaching, leaving the addition of the peppercorns and the vinegar (if any) until this time has elapsed. Then **simmer again** for a further 10 minutes.

MEAT

Beef

Lamb

Pork

THE MEAT RECIPES

Amongst the meat recipes are examples of dishes true to the cooking styles of their respective regions, using the ingredients traditionally provided in East Suffolk or in Provence.

Suffolk is rather more of a red meat part of the world than Provence. There is a strong emphasis on beef and pork in the East of England in addition to excellent poultry, although good lamb, and mutton too, is available from top quality producers. Stews made with pork and apple are part of the traditional fare.

In Provence the cooking is dominated by the superb Mediterranean fish and locally grown fruit and vegetables. Although meat dishes tend to be overshadowed by fish and poultry, Provence is nevertheless widely known for its Sisteron lamb which has EU Protected Geographical Indication (PGI). The characteristic stews of the region, the daubes, are important in everyday cooking and are made with a wide variety of meats including beef, lamb, wild boar and other furred game, often making full use of the magnificent supply of vegetables.

Amongst the other recipes in this chapter are English dishes influenced by the use of olive oil, red wines and herbs of Provence, and, of course, by the liberal use of tomatoes and garlic. These types of dishes bring together most effectively the cooking styles of the two regions.

All the recipes are easy to do and present no difficulties to those learning to cook in a methodical manner. I have found that the panic button in the kitchen is at long last gathering dust now that I am better organised, and all the ingredients for whatever I am about to make are brought together beforehand in a line like soldiers so that everything is readily to hand. The previous muddles were indescribable!

DAUBE À LA PROVENÇALE
(PROVENÇAL BEEF STEW WITH TOMATOES)

This is a really excellent recipe for a beef stew which is made very largely from beef and tomatoes. It takes very little time to put together. The stew is cooked for a very long time at a low oven temperature, and the delicious juice it creates during the cooking is produced entirely from the ingredients. No stock or other liquid is added, yet the end result is a beautifully succulent dish.

The stew needs only an inexpensive cut of beef. Chuck or shin is ideal.

Ingredients (Serves 3)
500g of beef chuck, diced into bite sized pieces
800g of medium sized tomatoes, quartered but not peeled
1 white onion, quartered
4 rashers of back bacon
6 or more good sized cloves of garlic, peeled
a handful of black olives, pitted
3 bay leaves, 3 sprigs of rosemary and a small bunch of thyme

Preheat the oven to Gas 1/2, 120C.

Quarter the onion and the tomatoes. **Cut** the bacon into small pieces. **Combine** all the ingredients in a heavy, lidded casserole over a low heat. Ensure the ingredients are well mixed and the olives free of stones. Warm it all thoroughly before putting the casserole in the oven.

Cook for six hours, stirring the ingredients every two hours or so. Ensure that the temperature of the oven stays constant – it is important to retain the moist nature of the stew.

Wine suggestion: A Syrah from the Rhône valley or alternatively a red from the Pays d'Oc in South West France.

SUFFOLK BEEF STEW

Stews are very much a matter of one's own personal style and contain whatever you fancy to make a nutritious and attractive dish. For example, if you dislike peppers leave them out. If you prefer celeriac, put some in. A mix of very slowly cooked meat and fresh vegetables can hardly go wrong. There are one or two keys to success, however. Do not stint on the red wine or the herbs, and be liberal with the garlic. As in game stews, the quantities should be very much your own. Your own stew is the best stew for you, so please treat the following as suggestions rather than directions although they do produce a good result.

Ingredients (Serves 3)
500g of diced beef, chuck (or shin which needs longer cooking)
2 large onions, chopped into rings
5 large fresh tomatoes, chopped, and a tin of chopped tomatoes
2 firm eating apples, quartered
2 large carrots, peeled and chopped into rings
½ a yellow pepper, cleaned and sliced into narrow strips
1 tablespoon of Balsamic vinegar
250 ml of robust red wine
1 heaped teaspoon of dried English herbs
a good teaspoonful of roughly ground black pepper
olive oil
7 fat garlic cloves, peeled and chopped

Preheat the oven to Gas 1, 140C.

Brown the peeled and chopped garlic and onions gently in olive oil in a heavy lidded casserole. **Add** the beef, the fresh and tinned tomatoes, and cover with red wine. Then **add** the prepared apple and the remaining vegetables. Then **add** the balsamic vinegar, herbs and pepper and **stir**. **Cook** for at least 3 hours.

Wine suggestion: a lusty country red from South West France such as Corbières.

DAUBE AUX PRUNEAUX (BEEF STEW WITH PRUNES)

This is a sensationally satisfying and warming stew, and although long, slow cooking is needed it can be put together in minutes. The recipe is a traditional French country recipe, probably from the South West so as to use the wonderful prunes from Agen. Slowly cooked so as to get every scrap of flavour from the beef, and peppery too, the ingredients marry beautifully. The wine to be incorporated needs to be a strong, robust country red but nothing too sophisticated. A sunny and well-structured red from Buzet on the South West banks of the River Garonne will match perfectly and especially with prunes from Agen. This is one of my favourite of all meat dishes.

Ingredients (Serves 4)
500g of beef (preferably grass-fed) diced into 4cm cubes (chuck steak is ideal)
200g of carrots, after having been peeled, and cut into short chunks
200g of onions, after having been peeled, and quartered
100g of pitted prunes
¾ bottle of robust red wine
2 bay leaves
seasoning

Preheat the oven to Gas Slow, 120C.

Cut the carrots into short chunks and peel and quarter the onions. **Combine** the beef with the vegetables and cover with wine in a heavy lidded casserole. Bring to a **simmer** on a gas ring or hotplate, and then place the casserole in the oven and **cook slowly** for a good 4 hours.

Remove from the oven and **add** salt and 2 bay leaves, and allow to **cool** and **marinate** in the lidded casserole for up to 24 hours. Refrigerate if necessary.

The next day **add** the prunes and **reheat** up to a simmer. **Add** pepper to taste, and continue to **simmer gently** for an hour. Serve with boiled potatoes.

Wine suggestion: Buzet, a red from South West France near Agen.

COTTAGE PIE

Cottage pie is made with beef, whereas shepherds pie is made with lamb. They are otherwise more or less the same. They are easy to make but can be dull. This recipe gives cottage pie more 'go'. I like to add garlic, balsamic vinegar, olive oil and plenty of herbs. Serve with peas, leeks or broccoli.

Ingredients (Serves 4)
500g of minced beef
600g of peeled potatoes, cooked and mashed
1 tin of chopped tomatoes
2 small shallots, finely chopped
100 ml of beef stock
4 garlic cloves, peeled and finely chopped
1 tablespoon of balsamic vinegar
a splash of olive oil
1 egg
English herbs
seasoning

Preheat the oven to Gas 6, 200C.

Boil the potatoes until soft. **Brown the mince** in a frying pan and let the fat run off and discard it. Transfer the meat to a saucepan. **Prepare** the stock and **stir it into** the beef together with the chopped tomatoes and also the finely chopped garlic and shallots. **Add** the herbs, the balsamic vinegar and the olive oil. **Heat** the saucepan gently, season the mixture and stir. Remove any surplus liquid. Then transfer to a high-sided pâté dish for baking.

Mash the boiled potatoes using a little warmed milk, or butter, and cover the beef thickly. **Glaze** by breaking the egg into a bowl, mixing the yolk and white together roughly, and spreading the egg on top of the mashed potato using a pastry brush. **Bake** for 30 minutes.

Wine suggestion: an unsophisticated red wine will suit well, such as Corbières.

ROAST LEG OR SHOULDER OF LAMB

I have consulted many sources to try to find the best advice for roasting prime cuts of lamb but every writer seems to have a different idea. At least I know that my own method works extremely well.

I have wondered why there are so many different ideas. The variables start with the hardware; cooking by town gas, bottled gas, electricity or solid fuel, or whether an oven is fanned or not, all create differences in both temperature and humidity. The temperature of the joint when it is introduced to the oven will differ. Whereabouts in the oven the joint is placed may also have a significant effect. The age and quality of the meat is relevant too.

Ingredients (Serves 4)
A leg of lamb on the bone, or shoulder, of approximately 850g
6 garlic cloves, peeled and shaped into spikes
olive oil

Preheat the oven to Gas 7, 220C.

Ensure the joint is at **room temperature**; this is most important. Shape the garlic cloves into spikes and **insert** them in the meat wherever possible.

Brush the joint all over with olive oil.

Roasting time is 25 minutes per 450g (1lb) and 25 minutes over. The **first 15 minutes** should be at **Gas 7, 220C**, and the **remainder** at **Gas 5, 190C**.

The meat is attractive to eat when pink in the centre. The probe should settle at around 72C.

Wine suggestion: any good Bordeaux but use the best you have.

Glemham cornfields

BARNSLEY LAMB CUTLETS WITH BUTTER BEANS

This is a simple little dish which is well balanced in every respect and extremely easy to do. Its pretty colouring on the plate is appealing and this can be made more attractive still by adding a bright green fresh vegetable such as garden peas or broccoli. The variety of tastes and texture is good too. I prefer to roast the cutlets rather than grill them. Ensure that the meat you buy comes from an animal butchered so as to produce true Barnsley cutlets.

Ingredients (Serves 2)
2 Barnsley lamb cutlets
80–100g of butter beans
2 large tomatoes prepared à la Provençale★

To grill the cutlets: **warm up** the grill for the cutlets and **preheat** the oven to Gas 7, 220C for the tomatoes.

Prepare the tomatoes **à la Provençale★**. They will be baked in the oven for 30 minutes, to be ready when the grilling has finished. Now **prepare** the organic butter beans draining and rinsing them. Then **heat them gently** on the hob with a knob of butter for a few minutes before the meat is ready (if using dried beans take account of the long preparation time, as explained in the Vegetable chapter★). **Trim** any excess fat from the cutlets.

The cutlets will need about 4–5 minutes on each side under the grill, according to your own preferences and the strength of the grill. A considerable amount of fat will be produced by the grilling, so ensure that it does not catch light.

To roast the cutlets: **preheat** the oven to Gas 7, 220C.

Prepare the butter beans as above. Then **start** to roast the tomatoes. They will need 30 minutes, which is 10 minutes longer than the time needed to roast the cutlets. Trim any excess fat from the cutlets and place them with the tomatoes in the oven (which have already been cooking for 10 minutes) to roast for 20 minutes. **Reduce the heat** to Gas 5, 190C for the final five minutes. Use a trivet on which to place the meat to ensure the fat falls away.

Wine suggestion: St. Chinian red from the Languedoc, North West of Beziers.

★ *Tomatoes à la Provençale, p.202; Boiling beans, p.191*

LAMB SHANKS

This is a wonderfully warming dish where long slow cooking produces really tender meat that simply falls off the bone. A shank per person gives a large portion which goes ideally with root vegetables. Lamb shanks may not always be immediately available and so remember to ask the butcher for them a day or two in advance.

Ingredients (Serves 2)
2 lamb shanks
4 good sized carrots, peeled and cut into chunks
1 large white onion, peeled and quartered
450ml of robust red wine
a splash of Balsamic vinegar
6 garlic cloves, peeled and chopped
3 tablespoons of olive oil
mixed English herbs
black peppercorns
Maldon salt

Marinate the lamb in the wine, olive oil, balsamic vinegar, herbs, garlic and peppercorns for two hours before starting to cook. **Turn** the shanks over after an hour.

Preheat the oven to Gas ¾, 130C. **Cut** the carrots into good sized–chunks and quarter the onion. **Combine** all the ingredients together in a heavy lidded casserole. **Season** with salt. **Cook** for 3 hours.

Wine suggestion: Fitou or similar robust red wine from South West France.

LAMB RAGOÛT (À L'ANGLAISE)

The name of this dish causes some amusement. I suppose because it was the idea of how the French think the English like to stew their lamb or mutton, that is to say without browning the meat, and without garlic, olives or wine. But perhaps I am wrong and it truly was the way in which the French like to stew their lamb, but in a style they believe to be ours. However, I do think this recipe is greatly improved by making it far less English (whatever the French may think) and so I have added taste and colour. À l'Anglaise it is no longer.

Ingredients (Serves 3)
500g of lamb shoulder, carefully diced and trimmed
350g of potatoes, thinly sliced
1 carrot, peeled and thinly sliced
2 onions, thinly sliced
3 tomatoes, thinly sliced
500ml of meat stock
a handful of olives and of raisins
2 cloves of garlic, peeled
1 teaspoon of herbs of Provence
2 glasses of red wine

Preheat the oven to Gas 3, 160C. Carefully **trim** the lamb, cutting off all the pieces of fat and then **brown** it gently in a frying pan letting all surplus fat run off.

Gently **fry** the garlic in olive oil in a lidded casserole and then place alternate layers of lamb and vegetables in the casserole. **Pour** in two glasses of red wine and just enough meat stock to cover the whole.

Add the olives, raisins and herbs. Replace the casserole lid and **bake** for at least two hours or until the potatoes and carrots are soft. Transfer to a serving dish and scatter with flat leaf parsley.

Wine suggestion: Morgon, or another leading Beaujolais cru.

LAMB AND FLAGEOLET BEANS

This easy supper dish can be made with either diced or minced lamb or alternatively with beef. Ensure the quality of the meat is good and as free from fat as possible, particularly if using lamb. It is an excellent dish for the true beginner as quantities can be left very much to one's own taste.

Ingredients (Serves 3)
500g of lamb (or beef), diced or minced
2 white onions, roughly chopped
500g of fresh tomatoes, chopped
1 tin of organic flageolet beans, washed
1 tablespoon of balsamic vinegar
1 dessertspoon of good red wine vinegar
½ a lemon, squeezed
2 glasses of red wine
dried English herbs
5 garlic cloves, peeled and chopped
ground black pepper

Wash the beans in a sieve under a cold tap and put on one side. **Gently brown** the two roughly chopped onions and the garlic cloves in olive oil using a large open but lidded pan. Cut off any surplus fat and gently **warm** the meat in a frying pan. Tip the pan and **discard** the excess fat which runs off the meat. Keep an eye on the onions so that they do not overcook.

Combine the meat with the onions in the open pan, and put it back on the heat. **Add** the tomatoes, then the beans. **Pour** on the two vinegars and lemon juice. **Pour** on two glasses of red wine. **Scatter** the herbs and season with black pepper and stir. Let it all **bubble gently** for 45 minutes. You may need to replace the lid of the open pan to retain some of the moisture in the dish.

Wine suggestion: A French country red such as Rasteau.

DICED SHOULDER OF MUTTON STEWED IN REAL ALE

In recent decades the popularity of mutton declined to the point where major efforts, notably by the Prince of Wales through his Mutton Renaissance initiative, have had to be made to revive its faded fortunes. This is in sharp contrast to the tastes of centuries past when mutton was very much a pleasure.

Mutton is simply sheep meat over two years old, yet the public perception is that of an old, tough and not very flavoursome meat. This is quite untrue of good mutton which, with age on its side, is more flavoursome than lamb and is both rich in nutrients and well balanced in the essential fatty acids, Omega-6 and Omega-3.

This inexpensive meat repays long, slow cooking, a technique which is unfashionable in our ever more hectic C21 lives, yet a mutton stew can be cooked at such a slow pace and for so long that there is endless opportunity for hectic activity during the six hours or so that is needed for this simple stew to work its magic. This is a particularly delicious recipe.

Ingredients (Serves 3 to 4)

500g of shoulder of mutton, diced
1 medium onion, finely chopped
500ml bottle of real ale
3 tomatoes, quartered (or the equivalent in baby tomatoes, halved)
1 tablespoon of tomato purée
6 garlic cloves, peeled and chopped
3 medium carrots, peeled and chopped into rings

2 sprigs of rosemary, freshly cut
4 sprigs of thyme, freshly cut
1 teaspoon of dried English herbs
a pinch of mace
½ teaspoon of roughly ground black pepper
salt

Preheat the oven to Gas 1/2, 120C.

Quickly **brown** the mutton in a dry frying pan, and discard the excess fat. In a heavy lidded casserole fry the chopped onion and garlic very gently in olive oil until the onions discolour. Then **add** the mutton, tomatoes and carrots and cover with ale. Now **add** the rest of the ingredients and stir.

Place in the cool oven for **six hours**, but after three hours add some ale if more liquid is needed to keep the meat moist. **Serve decorated** with flat parsley.

Wine suggestion: no wine – English real ale.

SUFFOLK PORK AND APPLE STEW

This unsophisticated recipe is very much one from the Suffolk countryside, although appropriate anywhere the pork is good and the apples are plentiful. A good supply of local dry cyder is particularly useful.

A good cut of pork makes the dish. A lean piece of loin carefully diced will produce a much better result than a cheaper or fattier cut.

Ingredients (Serves 3 to 4)
500g of pork loin, diced into 2–3cm cubes
1 large onion, sliced
2 Bramleys, or firm eating apples, peeled, cored and quartered
4 potatoes, peeled and halved
dry Suffolk cyder as needed to cover the contents of the casserole
fresh thyme, rosemary and plenty of sage

Preheat the oven to Gas 7, 220C.

Gently **fry** the onion slices in olive oil in a lidded casserole so that the onion discolours. Then remove the casserole from the heat. Now **brown** the pork in a frying pan so that the excess fat runs off. **Discard** the fat and **combine** the pork with the onion in the casserole and cover with dry cyder. Peel and halve the potatoes and **add** them to the casserole together with the quartered apples.

Now **add** the herbs, with plenty of sage, and **season**.

Place the casserole in the oven for 15 minutes at this high temperature.

Now **reduce the oven to Gas 2, 150C**. Cook at this cool temperature for 100 minutes. Serve with garden peas.

Wine suggestion: no wine – Aspall's Premier Cru Suffolk Cyder.

Pigs on the hill

BAKED PORK STEAKS MARINATED IN RED WINE AND HERBS

This is a rather delicious way of enjoying pork. It makes a dish which is full of character but one which is easy to prepare.

It is essential to buy really excellent and totally lean pork steaks. They will have been cut from the loin and de-boned by the butcher and, with the fat removed from the edge, will make a nugget of completely lean and tender meat. Much flavour and interest can be added with a marinade of English herbs and good red wine.

Ingredients (Serves 2)
2 pork steaks of about 130g each
for the marinade:
3 tablespoons of red wine
3 tablespoons of olive oil
1 dessertspoon of Balsamic vinegar
1 tablespoon of Merlot vinegar, or other good quality red wine vinegar
1 teaspoon of dried English herbs
4 good sized garlic cloves, crushed
ground black pepper

For **four hours before** cooking the pork steaks, immerse them in a mix of all the ingredients for the marinade. If there is insufficient liquid to cover the meat, turn the steaks once an hour. **When ready, preheat** the oven to Gas 6, 200C.

Save the marinade to make the sauce. Now bake the steaks for 30 minutes.

To prepare the sauce: having removed the excess oil from the marinade with a pipette or separator, **reduce** the remainder substantially over a moderate heat. Pour it over the steaks when ready to serve.

Wine suggestion: a simple Grenache from the Luberon.

PORK TENDERLOIN STUFFED WITH PRUNES

A tenderloin is the choicest pork cut and has the wonderful advantage of being entirely lean. It can be extremely enjoyable roasted after having been marinated in red wine, olive oil and herbs, but is more appealing still when a little stuffing is there to complement it. The simple stuffing I like, and which requires no preparation other than cutting into small pieces, is made entirely from prunes.

Ingredients (Serves 2)
1 pork tenderloin
prunes, tinned and stoned, diced finely, and their juice

for the marinade:
red wine, olive oil, fresh thyme and prune juice

Slit the tenderloin lengthways using a sharp knife but not so deeply as to separate the halves completely. This slit will accommodate the diced prunes.

Marinate the tenderloin in three tablespoons of olive oil mixed with sufficient red wine to cover, seasoned with fresh thyme and a little black pepper. Leave it to marinate for at least three hours.

After that time, remove the pork from the marinade and put the marinade to one side for the sauce. **Preheat** the oven to Gas 6, 200C.

Dice the prunes finely so that they fill the slit comfortably. Close the two halves together and tie them with string. Retain the prune juice and keep to one side.

Roast for 30–35 minutes.

To prepare the sauce: from the marinade use a pipette to skim off as much of the olive oil as possible and reduce the remainder of the liquid over a moderate heat. When it has reduced, mix in two tablespoons of the prune juice left over from the tin. **Stir** the liquid into a very little flour to thicken the sauce. (Do not stir the flour into the juice as it risks becoming lumpy).

Red cabbage is a good accompaniment.

Wine suggestion: a light red wine from Touraine.

PORK LOIN STEAKS IN MILK

It is perhaps surprising that milk offers such a suitable medium in which to cook pork. It seems to impart mildness and tenderness to a powerful meat yet milk suits it remarkably well. With the addition of garlic, sage and other herbs, and potatoes, it makes a warming dish for a cold day. It is extremely easy to prepare. It is cooked slowly at a modest temperature.

Ingredients (Serves 2)
2 pork loin steaks, trimmed and free of fat
a knob of butter
6 garlic cloves, peeled and halved
sage (fresh if available), thyme and nutmeg
450ml of milk (1 pint)
lemon zest cut into strips
8 potatoes of around 50g each having been peeled, left whole
seasoning

Preheat the oven to Gas 3, 160C.

In a casserole, **brown** the pork in olive oil. Then discard the oil used to brown the meat and put the meat to one side. In the already warm casserole melt a little butter and **brown** the garlic and **add** the thyme and sage.

Return the pork to the casserole and **pour** on all the milk. **Add** the lemon zest strips, and the nutmeg. Fit the potatoes round the pork steaks in the casserole and then season.

Now put baking paper over the rim of the casserole and secure the paper in position by replacing the lid.

Bake for 120 minutes

Wine suggestion: a wine from Burgundy such as a white Macon.

POULTRY

THE POULTRY RECIPES

Poultry is important both in Suffolk and Provence, and there are doubtless thousands of recipes in existence. Chicken is the perfect low-calorie food and, so long as the chicken is truly free-range and the birds have been properly treated and fed well, it is always enjoyable. The following recipes alternate between the traditions of Suffolk and the traditions of Provence but, as is the case throughout the book, a little of the Mediterranean has been injected into familiar English dishes where practicable whereas others are true representations of the cuisine of Provence.

I have used either whole chickens or chicken fillets throughout these very straightforward recipes. Chicken breasts are always the gold standard, leaving the legs (which can and should be a bit tough if the birds have been able to roam freely) for other recipes, and the wings which are fine for stock if you have the time or the inclination to make it (which hardly anyone does) and soup.

So much of the duck found in Britain is intensively farmed that few true farmyard ducks find their way on to the butchers' counters, but it is always a revelation to taste a "real walkabout duck". It is well worth seeking out the birds which have had a genuine outdoor life.

A recipe for roasting a whole guinea fowl has not been included as the preparations for whole roast chicken or a whole roast guinea fowl are more or less identical. However, guinea fowl is more flavourful than chicken and it is nice to feel able to cook it. Accordingly I have included a simple recipe for guinea fowl breasts which came to me as I was standing in the butcher's shop. The result is a delight, so do try it. It is extraordinarily easy, and all you have to do to achieve it is to wrap the breasts in prosciutto, make an orange sauce★ and roast for fifty minutes.

Once one has understood the Provençal way of doing things, expecting garlic, olive oil, lemons, tomatoes and herbs to turn up round virtually every corner, learning to cook in this style becomes almost second nature. The perfumes and savours float around almost telling you what to do next and the worries of those early days on the cookery road, so familiar to us all, dreamily melt away.

★ *Orange sauce, p.219*

CHICKEN BREASTS WITH GARLIC IN WHITE WINE

This dish is all about aromatics and very simple to prepare. White wine or dry cyder (wine is preferable but cyder is good) are excellent cooking liquids which blend perfectly with the traditional Provençal herbs and help to emphasise the savours of the garlic, rosemary, thyme and bay. Use a whole head of garlic, i.e. the whole bulb but carefully peel each clove.

Use a heavy lidded casserole. This will ensure that the chicken emerges beautifully moist and tender and the full benefit of the herbs will be retained. The cooking liquid makes a light and tasty sauce.

Ingredients (Serves 2)
2 good sized chicken breasts, skinned
1 good sized head of garlic, each clove carefully peeled
500ml of dry white wine (or dry cyder, Aspall's if available)
1 flat teaspoon of ground black pepper
fresh thyme if available, dried if not
2 sprigs of rosemary
3 bay leaves

Preheat the oven to Gas 3, 160C.

Peel the garlic cloves carefully, finishing up with at least eight good, fat cloves. Keep them whole, but ensure that their papery skin has been completely removed.

If the chicken fillets are very large, divide each of them into three. **Place** them with the garlic in the lidded casserole, pour on the wine, and put the casserole on the hob to warm up. **Add** the pepper, thyme, rosemary and bay.

Once the contents of the casserole are hot (remember to replace the lid), put it in the oven and cook for 90 minutes.

Nothing more need be done until it is ready. Serve with whatever vegetables you choose. Carrots are a successful accompaniment.

Wine suggestion: a white Viognier from the Pays d'Oc in South West France.

SUFFOLK CHICKEN STEW

There are endless recipes for chicken stew. This is real Suffolk – straightforward, scrumptious and successful. With few ingredients and no airs and graces, a delicious and warming dish is a certainty.

Ingredients (Serves 2/3)
2 chicken breasts, skinned and halved
12 large button mushrooms, halved
3 good size carrots, peeled, and chopped into large pieces
250ml of dry Suffolk cyder
dried English herbs and some fresh thyme if available
ground black pepper
olive oil
Maldon salt

Preheat the oven to Gas 3, 160C.

Chop the carrots into large pieces and **halve** the mushrooms and **sweat** them in a very little olive oil for a few minutes in a frying pan. Do not let them brown or burn.

Cover the bottom of a heavy lidded casserole with olive oil and, on a medium heat, **brown** the halved chicken breasts all over. As soon as the chicken has browned, **half-cover** them with dry cyder (make sure it is dry and not sweetened in any way, least of all with saccharine which **avoid like the plague**).

Add the carrots and mushrooms with all their cooking juices. **Sprinkle** liberally with the herbs and season with ground black pepper and a pinch of sea salt.

Put the lid on the casserole and cook in the oven for 90 minutes.

Wine suggestion: a structured red from the Right Bank, such as Fronsac.

COQ_AU VIN

The cockerel cooked in wine is as French as the blue beret, and, like the Suffolk chicken stew, there are endless recipes varying in complexity. Prepared in every corner of France, coq au vin varies in style, but I enjoy this simple and straightforward interpretation from the South of France.

First, do not worry whether the meat is from a chicken or a cockerel, if indeed you know. Fresh free range chicken fillets, skinned, will be admirable; the cockerel will be a little tougher. Secondly, decide whether you want to use red or white wine for the cooking. A Rhône red or a country white from the Languedoc will do splendidly.

Ingredients (Serves 2)
2 chicken fillets, skinned
100g of fresh mushrooms after having been peeled, sliced
75g of bacon, cut into small pieces
1 medium sized onion, sliced
400–500ml of red or white wine
fresh rosemary, thyme, sage and bay – or otherwise dried herbs of Provence

Preheat the oven to Gas 3, 160C.

Slice the onion and **cut up** the bacon. Cover the base of a lidded casserole with olive oil, **add** the onion and bacon, and start to **brown** them gently. **Halve the chicken** fillets, **add** them to the onion and bacon, and brown lightly. **Add** the wine, but do not quite cover the contents. **Add** the herbs.

Place in the oven and cook for about 80 minutes. At the end of this time **slice** the mushrooms, add them to the casserole and cook everything together for a further 15 minutes.

Serve with a bright green vegetable and potatoes sautéed with garlic.

Wine suggestion: For coq au vin rouge – Châteauneuf-du-pape, rouge.
For coq au vin blanc – a white from Languedoc.

A SIMPLE ROAST CHICKEN

Boiling an egg is simple. But can you roast a chicken? Well, of course, nothing is easier. Yet the methods used give rise to controversy and some cooks are wholly persuaded by the merits of how they feel it should be done.

It is said that the Duchess of Cornwall is adamant that a chicken for roasting should be stuffed with a whole lemon. If that is correct I totally agree with her. The result will certainly be a better, more succulent roast chicken, but there are other little techniques as well, such as the careful use of butter, herbs and garlic. All these things together will help to make a delicious roast bird.

> **Ingredients (Serves 4)**
> 1 organic free range chicken of around 1.7kg *(but note that the size of chickens is often measured in Imperial and traditional cooking times are often per pound)*
> 1 lemon, unwaxed
> 4 garlic cloves, skinned
> 2 slivers of cold butter
> thyme and seasoning

Preheat the oven to Gas 6, 200C.

Remove the bag of giblets, if any. **Trim** the lemon, cutting a thin slice off each end and make slits in the skin. **Insert** it into the cavity. Under the loose skin, especially around the breast, **insert** garlic cloves, thyme and small slivers of cold butter. Lightly brush the chicken all over with olive oil and **season** liberally with salt and black pepper.

Roast for 20 minutes a pound (454g) and 20 minutes over. On removal from the oven test with a probe to ensure 78C has been reached (it is always wise to ensure that a chicken, or other poultry, is properly cooked all through and that there is no sign of blood or pinkness).

Leave the chicken to stand for a few minutes before carving.

Wine suggestion: A good chicken merits an excellent red Burgundy such as a Savigny-lès-Beaune, or one of the best Beaujolais crus such as Brouilly.

CHICKEN AND CHORIZO À LA PROVENÇALE

This is a true country dish from Provence, full of flavour, releasing those mouth watering aromas that hit you so often as you walk along a village street in Provence on a hot morning before midday.

The important thing is to buy good quality chorizo. It is not unknown for so-called chorizo to contain horse and donkey to pad out the pork, or other meats you might not want to think about! The best known chorizo is Andalusian.

Ingredients (Serves 2/3)
2 free range chicken breasts, skinned and cut into chunks
½ a chorizo sausage, sliced
1 bulb of garlic, peeled
3 medium sized white onions, sliced
4 small courgettes, thickly sliced
4 fresh tomatoes, thickly sliced, and 1 tin of chopped tomatoes
½ a lemon, squeezed
200ml red wine
a handful of black olives, pitted
olive oil and dried herbs

Step 1: Slice the onions, courgettes and fresh tomatoes and peel the garlic. Lightly **fry** the garlic and sliced onions in olive oil using a wide-lidded pan. **Add** the tinned tomatoes. **Add** the sliced courgettes, the fresh tomatoes and the wine. **Simmer** the whole for about 40 minutes. This makes a simple ratatouille.

Step 2: Lightly brown the chicken chunks in oil and lemon juice in a frying pan. Then **combine** the chicken with the ratatouille. **Add** the herbs and season. **Simmer** the whole for at least 45 minutes but after 30 minutes **add** the olives.

Step 3: After adding the olives keep the ratatouille simmering. In a separate pan start to dry fry the chorizo. **Discard** the voluminous fat the chorizo produces. **Combine** everything together and **simmer** for the final five minutes.

Wine suggestion: Côtes-du-Rhône-villages.

Keeping hens

ROAST SUFFOLK CHICKEN BREASTS WITH SUFFOLK PLUMS

Suffolk is very well known for both its poultry and its wonderful plums, and it seems highly appropriate to include this very appealing dish. Of course, chickens and plums can be found everywhere in England and in France too, so there is nothing more than a little romanticism in the name of the recipe. Naturally, all that is pretty irrelevant and what the cook wants to know is whether the dish is worthwhile. The answer to that is a resounding yes. It is quite straightforward to cook with a degree of enjoyment on the super-plus scale.

The chicken breasts are prepared in a plum marinade for three or four hours in advance, then roasted with the marinade and more plums for a little less than an hour.

Ingredients (Serves 2)
2 free range chicken breasts
500g of Victoria plums (or similar), stoned and quartered
1 medium-sized onion, roughly chopped
6 cloves of garlic, all skinned but two chopped and four left whole
3 tablespoons of olive oil
3 tablespoons of quality red wine vinegar
1 tablespoon of Demerara sugar
a good handful of crinkly or flat parsley, chopped
Maldon sea salt

To make the marinade: **Blend**, all together, using at least 100g of the plums, the vinegar, the olive oil, the sugar, the two chopped garlic cloves and half the chopped parsley. Season with salt. Pour the marinade over the chicken and leave for three or four hours, **basting** the chicken occasionally.

To cook the dish: **Preheat** the oven to Gas 6, 200C and remove the chicken from the marinade. **Cook** the onion and the remaining whole garlic cloves **very gently** in olive oil in a saucepan until they have discoloured a little. Then, in a small roasting tray, **place** the remainder of the plums, the lightly cooked whole garlic cloves and onion. **Place** the chicken on top and then **cover** the chicken thickly with the marinade – use it all – and season with salt.

Roast for 25 minutes. After this time **reduce** the oven to Gas 4, 180C for a further 25 minutes. When cooked, decorate with the remaining parsley.

Wine suggestion: Gewurztraminer from Alsace.

COLD CHICKEN BREASTS WITH TOMATO COULIS

This is a delicious summer lunch with a strong Provençal feel to it. The chicken needs to be of excellent quality and the tomatoes red and ripe.

The coulis is suitable for many dishes, but this one is really satisfactory and easily prepared. The chicken and the coulis make a perfect match.

Ingredients (Serves 2)
2 plump free range chicken breasts, skinned
herbs of Provence
4 or 5 large ripe tomatoes, peeled★
4 fat garlic cloves, crushed
½ lemon, squeezed
olive oil
Maldon salt

To cook the chicken breasts: **preheat** the oven to Gas 6, 200C.

Sprinkle a few herbs of Provence on the chicken breasts and **roast** them for 50–55 minutes. Remove them from the oven and **let them go cold**.

To make the coulis: **peel**★ the tomatoes and cut out the stalks. **Crush** the peeled tomatoes using a pestle and mortar if you have one, otherwise use a pudding bowl and a wooden spoon. **Crush** the garlic cloves and **stir** them into the tomatoes making a juicy mixture. **Add** the lemon juice. Now **add** a few drops of olive oil. **Salt** the mixture very lightly and ensure it has properly blended.

Pour the coulis over the chicken when ready to serve.

Wine suggestion: tomatoes always create difficulties. Try Beaujolais or a very young red from South West France.

★ *Peeling tomatoes, p.200*

SPATCHCOCK CHICKEN

A small chicken prepared *en crapaudine*, that is to say in French 'like a toad', is a traditional method of cooking chickens and pigeons, dating back for centuries. It has the great merit of allowing a whole bird to be cooked quite rapidly, especially if grilled as it always used to be done. However, I have discovered that roasting instead of grilling is very satisfactory, leaving the bird very well cooked but ensuring its juices remain concentrated. Whereas a whole chicken roasted in the traditional way can sometimes be rather dry, this method allows the meat to retain its succulence yet other flavours may easily be added.

Ask your butcher to spatchcock a small chicken weighing around 1.4–1.6kg. You may then season it as you wish using, for example, herbs, mustard and garlic. The recipe I suggest here is very enjoyable but it does not venture too far into the culinary imagination. It simply calls for olive oil, garlic, mustard and herbs of Provence, but there is a great deal of scope here for creativity.

Ingredients (Serves 2+)
1 spatchcocked chicken of around 1.5kg
olive oil
½ lemon cut lengthways
6 garlic cloves, peeled and finely chopped
1 dessertspoonful of herbs of Provence
a pinch of mustard powder

Preheat the oven to Gas 6, 200C.

Place the chicken in a roasting tin so that it can be fully spread–eagled. Lightly brush it all over with olive oil. Place the half-lemon, **skin down**, underneath.

Prepare a mixture of olive oil, finely chopped garlic, herbs of Provence and a little mustard powder and then brush it all over the chicken.

Roast for 75 minutes.

Wine suggestion: a red Lirac from the West bank of the Rhône.

CHICKEN SAUTÉ À LA PROVENÇALE

There are innumerable recipes for chicken sauté. There are doubtless many from Provence alone, but this one is easy and enjoyable. Like so much cooking which originates from the South of France, it leaves you satisfied yet with a sense of contentment and well-being rather than a legacy of over-indulgence.

For subtle variations in taste you may like to look at the recipe for Provençal sauce.

Ingredients (Serves 2)
2 free range chicken breasts, skinned and diced
5 good sized tomatoes, chopped
1 small onion, chopped
½ red pepper, de-seeded, cleaned and narrowly sliced
a good handful of black olives, pitted
5 garlic cloves, chopped finely
olive oil
herbs of Provence
seasoning

Preheat the oven to Gas 1, 140C.

Chop the tomatoes, onion and garlic and put them aside. Keep the tomatoes separate. **Dice** the chicken and, in a casserole, **sauté** the pieces until lightly brown. Then **remove** them from the casserole and put them aside.

Lightly **fry** the chopped onion and garlic together in the casserole in the oil used to brown the chicken. When the onion starts to discolour, **add** the tomatoes and **stir** over a low heat. **Cut** the pepper into narrow strips and add them to the casserole. Now **add** the chicken and the olives. **Season** and **add** the herbs, warm through and stir ready for cooking. **Cook** for 75–80 minutes.

Wine suggestion: red Bandol from Provence.

ROAST DUCK BREASTS

This recipe started life as magret de canard, but after research and enquiry I reached the conclusion that a genuine magret is for another day. A magret is the breast of a force fed Mallard or Pekin duck (which may or may not be a process to one's taste) but whatever opinion is held there are so many complicated recipes for it that I have opted for simplicity in true Suffolk style. The recipe which follows is both easy to prepare and delicious, but any roasted duck can be dry on its own, so a suitable sauce is worth its weight in gold. The orange sauce★ I created from ingredients which were ready to hand at the time, complements a roast duck rather well. I very much hope you will enjoy the dish as much as I do.

Ingredients (Serves 2)
2 breasts of duck with skin intact
olive oil
a knob of butter
fresh or dried thyme

Preheat the oven to Gas 6, 200C.

Make three shallow incisions in the skin of each breast. Cover the base of a frying pan with olive oil. Heat the oil and then introduce the breasts **skin side down** and **fry** them for about 5 minutes, **adding** a good knob of butter to the pan and a heaped teaspoon of dried or fresh thyme and basting the breasts a couple of times.

Now **transfer** the duck breasts to a lightly oiled roasting tray **skin side up** and **roast** for about 15 minutes for the meat to be medium done.

Serve with orange sauce★.

Wine suggestion: this dish merits a very good Bordeaux. Try one of my old favourites, Château Potensac from the Bas-Medoc.

★ *Orange sauce, p.219*

SIMPLE ROAST DUCK

Poultry is so much of a mass produced product that it has become more and more difficult to seek out birds which are truly free range (although not necessarily organic) and which are well kept and fed, and content. For chickens this is less difficult but for guinea fowl it is often quite a problem as so many are imported. Even in rural Suffolk one has to look quite hard to find a true farmyard duck which has lived a free ranging life. Whereas branded products raised on a large scale are widely distributed, a "proper walkabout duck", as my butcher calls them, are less easily found.

Although the right butcher with good farm contacts can provide an excellent bird, I have found that cookery books cannot be relied on either for simplicity or certainty to ensure a successful and simple roast.

My own recipe is not rocket science. However, it works beautifully, it could hardly be more straightforward and it will reward you with a delicious meal.

Ingredients (Serves 4)
1 'proper walkabout duck', farm bred and well fed of about 2.2kg (5lb)
1 small orange
orange sauce★

Preheat the oven to Gas 6, 200C.

Make incisions into the orange, cut off the ends and stuff it into the cavity of the duck. Brush the duck all over with olive oil, sprinkle it with salt and place it in a **deep roasting tray, on a rack, upside down**. **Roast** for 30 minutes.

Remove it from the oven, empty the tray of fat, turn the duck **breast side up**, and then roast for a further 90 minutes.

When the 90 minutes have expired, **turn the oven up** to Gas 8, 230C for 10 minutes to crisp up the skin. Then **remove** from the oven and leave for **10** minutes. Serve with mushrooms, sauté potatoes and orange sauce★.

Wine suggestion: Cahors from South West France.

★ *Orange sauce, p.219*

DUCK LEGS IN CYDER

Duck legs can be rather tough particularly if the bird has had an active life, so the legs need to be extremely well done to be really enjoyable. However, long, slow cooking in liquid transforms them and this simple recipe does produce a delicious supper dish. First, though, the legs must be skinned. It is a hard job unless you have the knack. Speaking from the miserable experience of trying to do the job myself it saves much heartache if the butcher will do it. Otherwise, think of the skin as a pair of tight jeans which you pull off from the waist!

Ingredients (Serves 2)
2 good sized duck legs, skinned
6 shallots, chopped
2 carrots, sliced
dry cyder, sufficient to (almost) cover the legs in the casserole
4 cloves of garlic, chopped
1 teaspoon of dried English herbs
black pepper
seasoning

Preheat the oven to Gas 3, 160C.

Chop the shallots and garlic finely. Cover the base of a heavy lidded casserole with olive oil and use it to **fry** the shallots and garlic **very gently** to the point that they discolour a little.

While the shallots and garlic are frying, **brown** the skinned duck legs in a little olive oil in an open frying pan over a moderate heat. This will burn off the unwanted surplus fat.

Now **add** the duck legs and carrots to the heavy casserole and **almost cover** them with cyder. **Season** with black pepper and a little salt, and **add** the dried herbs. Place the lid on the casserole and cook in the oven for about 2 hours.

Wine suggestion: a country red from the North of Provence such as Rasteau or Ventoux.

GUINEA FOWL BREASTS IN PROSCIUTTO WITH ORANGE SAUCE

Surveying the butcher's counter I came across some breasts of guinea fowl wrapped in streaky bacon. Considering them for a moment or two it struck me that the bacon could be improved upon by using thin slices of *prosciutto di Parma*. Furthermore the breasts had not been skinned and would therefore produce much more fat than I would like. I thought the answer would be to remove the skin and coat the breasts lightly all over with olive oil, possibly flavoured with a little garlic, then to roll up the breasts in thin slices of the ham. I thought that an orange sauce would complement both the guinea fowl and the ham. The result was a little stunner, so here it is...!

Ingredients (Serves 2)
2 breasts of guinea fowl, skinned
4 thin slices of prosciutto di Parma
olive oil, flavoured with garlic if wished
orange sauce★

Preheat the oven to Gas 6, 200C.

Lightly oil a roasting tray. Also coat the breasts lightly with olive oil and **roll** them up in the slices of ham. Do not allow the ham to overlap too much. Place the breasts (which are now rolled up in the ham) in the roasting tray.

Roast for 50 minutes.

Using the recipe in this book **prepare an orange sauce★**. This can always be done in advance although there is ample time to achieve this while the guinea fowl is roasting.

Wine suggestion: A Chinon from Touraine or a red Saumur.

★ *Orange sauce, p.219*

GAME

Feathered

Furred

A mixed bag

GAME SEASONS
IN ENGLAND

Grouse . . . . 12th August – 10th December

Pheasant . . . . 1st October – 1st February

Partridge . . . . 1st September – 1st February

Pigeon . . . . No close season

Wild Duck . . . . 1st September – 31st January

Deer . . . . July – February
(subject to species and gender)

Rabbit . . . . No close season

Hare . . . . Not to be sold: 1st March – 31st July

THE GAME RECIPES

In common with the recipes throughout this book the recipes for game are simple and straightforward to execute. The rationale behind the selection is to enable the budding cook to achieve at least one attractive dish for each game bird or animal, which will make a good start towards establishing his or her own repertoire.

The most commonly shot game bird is undoubtedly the pheasant, for which two recipes are included, one roast and one stew. Partridge, which is also widely available, is included as a roast, because it is so delicious cooked that way. Pigeon is, in France, traditionally served with peas, reputedly because Louis XIV liked peas with pigeons. Pigeon breasts can be bought very cheaply and, with a little imagination, can be used in a wide variety of ways throughout the year as there is no close season. If whole pigeons are preferred, it is good to roast them spatchcocked in the traditional French manner. However, wild duck is much less common. Unless you go down to the cold marshes of the River Deben or another of the great East Anglian rivers at dusk, and wait patiently as the silvery, glugging rivulets fill with muddy water on the incoming tide, with a 12 bore at your side, supplies are limited.

In Suffolk good rabbits can be acquired by most butchers, but the really wonderful venison from the forests close to the Suffolk coasts can produce truly memorable meals once one learns from whom to buy it and how best to cook it.

I have not included hare amongst the game. Although undoubtedly very good to eat, and the subject of many excellent recipes, the hare is such a beautiful animal and of such grace that I cannot bring myself to propose it here. The Brown Hare is much less prolific than it used to be in England, and whenever I see a hare, ears erect and with that central nervous system on high alert, ready to react with the speed of a lightning flash and sprint into the distance I cannot but admire a truly noble creature.

ROAST PHEASANT AND BACON

Choose a good, plump bird, and one which has been cleanly shot and not mutilated by an ill-trained spaniel or peppered to pieces at short range. Look for a bit of fat too, as this helps to keep the bird moist during roasting.

Many people prefer a hen rather than a cock bird, as they maintain the flavour is better although it is not always possible to tell when you are buying an oven-ready bird. Go for a nice, plump specimen, but avoid that tough old cock bird that had evaded the guns for years!

The key to a nicely roasted bird is to keep it moist during cooking. One way of doing this is to lubricate it all over with olive oil before you start, and then to drape it with a bacon rasher or two during the second half of the roasting. If you put the bacon on at the beginning, it will have blackened by the end and will not be edible.

Ingredients (Serves 2)
1 pheasant, oven ready
1 or 2 rashers of reasonably fatty bacon
olive oil

Roasting should take **about 45 minutes** depending on size and weight. The bird needs to be fully cooked and reach a **probe temperature of 75C**.

Preheat the oven to its **maximum temperature**.

The moment you have placed the pheasant in the oven reduce the temperature to Gas 5, 190C and keep it at that temperature. After 25 minutes **trickle** olive oil over the bird and drape the bacon over the breast.

Roasted winter vegetables are an excellent accompaniment, especially parsnips.

Serve with game sauce★.

Wine suggestion: a well structured red such as Cahors or, ideally, a red Burgundy.

★ *Game sauce, p.211*

PHEASANT STEW WITH APPLES, LENTILS AND ROSEMARY

This dish is the very epitome of Autumn in Suffolk or anywhere in rural England – pheasant, new season's apples and freshly pressed cyder. Totally straightforward to do, it is a wonderful way to draw the flavours out of the bird and the fruit. Try to find good sized eating apples which cook well and which have a fresh, sharp character rather than apples that are soapy or sweet. Crispins are ideal. This dish benefits from slow cooking, and if you have a tough old cock bird give it half an hour longer.

Ingredients (Serves 2)
1 pheasant, oven ready (or 2 large pheasant breasts, skinned)
6 button onions, trimmed; or 3 shallots, halved
6 small mushrooms, halved
3 good sized eating apples, peeled, cored and quartered
200g of Puy lentils, ready cooked
3 sprigs of rosemary
3 cloves of garlic, chopped
olive oil
dry Suffolk cyder, sufficient to cover the pheasant

Preheat the oven to Gas 3, 160C.

First, **trim** the onions, **chop** the garlic, and wash the lentils. **Peel and quarter one half** of the apples. Place all on one side. Cover the base of a heavy, lidded casserole with olive oil and **brown** the pheasant all over.

Now **add** just the onions and chopped garlic and lightly **stir fry** them with the pheasant for two minutes in the casserole. Then **add** enough cyder to cover the pheasant. **Add** the lentils, rosemary and the apples you have already peeled.

Place the stew in the oven and **cook** for 60 minutes (or 90 minutes for a tough old bird). **Peel** and **quarter** the remaining apples and after the 60 minutes **add** them to the stew with the mushrooms. **Cook** for a further 30 minutes.

Wine suggestion: no wine; Aspall's Suffolk draught cyder will be ideal.

ROAST PARTRIDGE

For many people (including me) partridge is the most delicious of the common game birds and is simplicity itself to cook. Many recipes require the birds to be roasted on one side, then on the other and finally the right way up. I am not persuaded that this is best and, especially when using a fan oven, am happy to leave the bird the right way up on a trivet throughout. Birds are often roasted covered with a rasher of bacon, although all they really need is to be well brushed with olive oil and well basted with cooking liquids during the roasting.

Partridge shooting starts in England on 1ˢᵗ September, a month earlier than for pheasants, and so in some years partridges are the first game birds to reach their best. November is perfect.

Ingredients (Serves 2)
1 oven ready partridge **per person**
a knob of butter
ground black pepper

Preheat the oven to its **maximum temperature**.

Roasting will take **about 35 minutes**, although if covered with bacon a little longer will be needed. The birds need to be fully cooked and **the probe should reach about 75C**.

Take a good knob of cold butter, roll it around in some black pepper and **insert** it in the cavity of each bird. **Brush** the birds all over with olive oil. **Place** the birds on a trivet in a roasting tray with **the breasts uppermost**.

Then **place them in the oven but the moment you have done so reduce** the **temperature to Gas 5, 190C**. Baste the birds well during the cooking, especially during the second half. Serve with redcurrant jelly or game sauce★.

Wine suggestion: a red from the Haut-Medoc in Bordeaux or from La Côte de Nuits in Burgundy.

★ *Game sauce, p.211*

TRIO OF PHEASANT, PARTRIDGE AND VENISON SAUSAGE

The credit for this most appealing combination for the game season is due to Paul and Dan at Creaseys (Butchers) of Peasenhall in Suffolk. The amalgamation of gamey tastes and the simplicity of the cooking is most attractive, and I have added a red wine sauce for game★ to complete the dish. Roast it with potatoes and a winter vegetable such as parsnip to complete the ensemble. Nothing will be more comforting. Have it on dark, windy and wintry nights before Christmas. Each serving will comprise one pheasant breast, one partridge breast and one wild venison sausage so you do need to be quite hungry.

Ingredients (Serves 2)
2 pheasant breasts, skinned
2 partridge breasts, skinned
2 wild venison sausages
red wine sauce for game★

Preheat the oven to Gas 7, 220C.

Lightly **oil** a roasting tray and also brush the meats lightly with olive oil.

Roast in a hot oven for 30–35 minutes. If the meat is tending to dry while cooking, **baste** with a little olive oil.

Wine suggestion: a generic Burgundy of good quality.

★ *Game sauce, p.211*

PIGEON BREASTS AND BACON ON A PURÉE OF GARDEN PEAS

In France, pigeon has traditionally been associated with peas which makes an excellent combination. The gastronomic match between pigeon and peas seems to have originated in the late C17 and this is thought to be due to the seriousness with which Louis XIV took his magnificent nine hectare vegetable garden at Versailles known as *le potager du roi*.

This simple dish brings pigeon and peas together on a bed of puréed garden peas, accompanied by a little bacon. The Suffolk version, which is also very good, is to substitute the purée of peas for a purée of creamed celeriac, made with a knob of butter and a dollop of low fat yoghurt.

Ingredients (Serves 2)
4 pigeon breasts, skinned and sliced in half or in thirds
10 tablespoons of peas, fresh or frozen
4 rashers of sweet-cure back bacon
garlic olive oil
1 knob of butter

Skin the pigeon breasts and slice them as flatly as possible. **Prepare** the bacon, removing the rind and surplus fat.

Pour boiling water over the peas and then boil them for a few minutes. Peas cook very quickly. Drain and keep warm.

In a large frying pan **sauté** the pigeon breasts very gently for a few minutes in garlic olive oil and a little butter. Once the breasts are warm, **add** the bacon and sauté over a medium heat until cooked through. The pigeon will cook in about the same time as is needed to cook the bacon.

Put a knob of butter with the peas, and **blend** into a purée.

Make a bed of peas on each plate and place the pigeon and bacon on top.

Wine suggestion: a red Touraine gamay from the Loire.

ROAST WILD DUCK BREASTS

This recipe brings you a little bit of real, truly natural Suffolk, and it is hoped that the pleasure of eating roast breast of wild duck will remain in your mind.

The county teems with wild duck, and I have the privilege of living in close proximity to many of them. As I write no less than twenty are peacefully sitting next to the water outside my window, serenely unaware that as the heat of the summer begins to fade life will soon be quite different. Once the duck shooting season starts on the first of September they will have abandoned their lazy repose by the waters edge in favour of moving from flight pond to flight pond, dodging those double-barrels at dusk, so devilishly intent on their demise!

These birds are mallards, although teal and widgeon may also be found on the River Alde as it dreamily wends its way closer to the sea, but mallards make good eating. Whereas the breasts may swiftly be roasted, the legs need much more time in the oven, and so I have cast them aside for this recipe. However, duck does need an interesting sauce, and although a red wine sauce for game★ will do, the other little bit of our county I want to bring you is the sauce made from the bullace, which ripens in November.

Ingredients (Serves 2)
2 breasts of wild duck (Mallard)
olive oil
bullace sauce★ (a plum sauce made in the same fashion may be substituted)

Preheat the oven to Gas 8, 230C.

Place the breasts **skin side up** in a roasting tray lightly oiled. Oil the breasts with olive oil and, ensuring the oven is right up to temperature, **roast** for 15 minutes.

Serve with a bullace (or plum) sauce★.

Wine suggestion: the best red wine from St. Emilion you can find.

★ *Game sauce, p.211; Bullace sauce, p.216;*

ROAST LOIN OF WILD VENISON

This very straightforward dish requires a most excellent butcher. You need to enquire when a top quality animal is about to come his way from a good source (ideally in December or January) because to be able to roast a really superb loin will be a culinary experience in itself and the game equivalent of that piscatorial revelation – the poached wild sea trout.

We are lucky in East Suffolk to have venison from Rendlesham forest or Dunwich at hand, although there are other places in the county and many in the British Isles where really good wild venison can be obtained.

One of the most important aspects of buying venison is to obtain meat from an animal that has been instantly and cleanly shot without suffering. Fear, pain and stress induce surges of adrenalin causing the muscles to tense, the meat to toughen and the taste to deteriorate. In any event no beast, domestic or wild, should be allowed to suffer at the hands of the farmer or hunter.

Ingredients (Serves 4)
800g of loin of venison
2 rashers of back bacon

Marinade: a tawny port or robust red wine to cover the meat, 1 tablespoon of good olive oil, 2 cloves of finely chopped garlic, ground black pepper and a few black peppercorns, a few juniper berries and some dried mixed herbs.

Marinate for at least four hours in an open porcelain dish just large enough to take the meat comfortably, thus economising on the ingredients.

Preheat the oven to Gas 8, 230C. **Remove** the venison from the marinade. **Dry** the venison, brush it with olive oil and place it in a roasting tray with the bacon on top. **Roast** for 10 minutes at Gas 8, 230C and then for about 13 minutes at Gas 4, 180C. The venison should reach an internal temperature of about 57C and be nicely pink in the centre. In the meantime, using a separator, draw off and discard the oil from the marinade and **reduce** the remainder for sauce.

A good accompaniment is a selection of winter vegetables together with some broccoli and a purée of potato and celeriac*.

Wine suggestion: A velvety Volnay from La Côte de Beaune (ideally), or a good red Burgundy.

---

* *Potato and celeriac purée, p.195*

WILD RABBIT STEW FROM PROVENCE

Wild rabbit stew is a traditional Provençal dish. Wild rabbits abound in the rocky terrain whereas in Suffolk they are a pest of field and hedgerow. Rabbit stew from the two regions has much in common and can be neatly summed up by the fact that, in Suffolk, Bramley apples and cyder feature strongly whereas in Provence prunes, wine, olives and tomatoes characterise the dish.

For either Provençal or Suffolk style ask the butcher to discard the forelegs and joint the remainder into four: each hind leg and the saddle crossways into two.

Ingredients (Serves 4)
2 rabbits, each jointed into 4; the hind legs; and each saddle crossways into 2
500ml (minimum) of dry white wine, ideally from Provence
8 shallots, peeled and chopped
6 carrots, peeled and cut into short lengths
100g black or green olives, pitted
18 prunes, stoned and halved
500g of tomatoes, chopped
400g of courgettes, peeled and cut into lumps
8 large garlic cloves, peeled and crushed
leaves of a small bunch of fresh thyme
seasoning

Preheat the oven to Gas 2, 150C. **Cover** the base of a **wide pan** with olive oil. Place it over a high heat and **brown** the rabbit joints. Now **cover** the base of a heavy lidded casserole with olive oil, **add** the shallots and garlic, and **warm** gently. **Add** the browned rabbit joints with their cooking juices and also the carrots. **Pour** in enough wine to cover the joints. **Add** the olives, prunes, tomatoes, courgettes and the herbs. Bring to a **simmer**. **Season**, and **stew** in the oven for about 3 hours. As a friend from Aix-en-Provence rightly says: "when the carrots are done the stew is done".

Wine suggestion: a red Buzet.

MIXED GAME STEW

I have developed this recipe over time and successive stews, and the lengthy list of ingredients, just in case it is putting you off, is well worthwhile.

Not all of us are fortunate enough to have abundant game close at hand, although there are still many parts of Britain and even more in France where a great deal of good game is found. This recipe is extremely useful in so far as it accommodates all types of game in whatever proportions are available or preferred. It can be used in season for a ready-prepared medley of game to include pheasant, partridge, pigeon, woodcock, duck, rabbit and venison in any combination.

Ingredients (Serves 2/3)
500g of mixed game in any proportion, diced
1 red and 1 white onion, sliced
7 good-sized garlic cloves, peeled and roughly chopped
1 tin of chopped tomatoes and 2 fresh tomatoes, chopped
250–300ml of robust red wine
a splash of good red wine vinegar
1 tablespoon of Balsamic vinegar
2 rashers of back bacon, chopped
1 Bramley apple, peeled, cored and quartered
2 pears, peeled, cored and quartered
olive oil
black peppercorns, crushed
fresh rosemary, bay, and thyme (with sprigs tied together)
dried basil
3 squares of 99% chocolate

Quantities may be widely varied with this recipe as it is good to develop a style of one's own. The game can include or exclude whatever you prefer and the other ingredients can casually be added in the proportions that suit in the hope that all will be well. Never fear – it will!

Preheat the oven to Gas ¾, 130C. **Cover** the base of a heavy lidded casserole with olive oil. **Slice** one red and one white onion and roughly chop the garlic cloves. **Sweat** the onions and garlic in the oil over a low heat **together with** the bacon.

When the onions begin to colour **add** the diced game mix and then cover it with a robust red wine. A third of a bottle should be sufficient. If you would prefer not to use a Burgundy an inexpensive wine from the Rhône valley will do well. **Maintain** a gentle heat and **add** a tin of chopped tomatoes, the fresh tomatoes, a quartered cooking apple, the quartered pears, a tablespoon of Balsamic vinegar, a splash of good red wine vinegar, the chocolate and some crushed black peppercorns. Finally **add** the herbs.

You will find throwing all this together such fun that you will not be agonising about precise quantities. This is *real* cooking!

Bring all to the boil, ensuring the ingredients are well mixed, and then place in the oven for about 3 hours. **Stir** every hour.

Wine suggestion: a full bodied red of your choice, whether an expensive Burgundy or a modest red from South West France such as Fitou in West Languedoc or Bergerac in the Dordogne.

Woodcock   Karen Freeman

WHAT MAKES
A TRUE COUNTRYMAN ?

I have often wondered what makes a true, really true, countryman. In this sophisticated age we could be forgiven for thinking that such people are figures from the past, mere relics of a former age, usually clad in a manner now forgotten with red spotted handkerchief round the neck, shotgun in hand, pheasants and partridges in a bulging game bag slung across the shoulder.

One can imagine such a character wending his way home after an autumn day's shooting. He will have with him, obediently to heel, his devoted black Labrador, both eager to return to the warmth of his cottage as dusk falls. His boots squelch in the mud and rustle the piles of wind blown leaves as he nears home and listens intently for flighting mallard before a formation comes into view silhouetted against the deepening blue night sky. As he reaches his door his mind turns to the cooking to be done which will give expression to his intuition and experience in the field.

The countryman we may have in our minds is not, though, just an imaginary figure from the past. Such countrymen are a breed. Without them we would be all the poorer.

I write as night falls and I can see him in my mind so clearly, but I can also hear the reality of the pheasants in the trees around the house. Those sounds remind me how the true countryman lives – so very close to nature – and I want to tell you about one who is an old and valued friend.

In Suffolk there are a number of great rivers, amongst them the River Deben that winds its way from Debenham in the middle of the county down to Woodbridge and onwards to the sea. In its tidal lower reaches it broadens, not only through the width of water but through the expanse of salt marshes along its banks, creating a panorama of immense open skies and riverscapes of rare beauty. Because of the extensive marshland the settlements along its banks are far from the water's edge and in one tiny village which nestles close to the marsh itself there is a small cottage I know well. That cottage is the home of one of those really true countrymen I have spoken about.

The cottage was built, I suppose, in the C17 and is reputed to have been one of many smugglers cottages where contraband, especially tobacco, was stored, having been imported with little fear of detection. From the river the smugglers' boats slid silently into the many creeks in the saltings where their cargoes were quietly unloaded, although finding the way at night was hazardous. In the C18 at Hemley Hall, on the port side of the river as you sail up to Woodbridge, a light shone from an upper window to guide the smugglers in. The cottage lies further downriver where the slope of the land starts to peter out and a track runs down to the marsh itself, making access to the river easier for both smuggler and wildfowler alike. There are wide views in all directions from the upper rooms, from which the river scene is staggeringly beautiful. It is from one of these upper rooms that you will see how the story unfolds.

Our countryman lives his life in his own little world and has very limited use for the trappings of modern life. His motor, an old and trusty Land-Rover, gives him all the mobility he needs. That all-weather vehicle never fails him. Unstoppable, uncomfortable, unimaginable without its owner and its dog bed, its straw, its tools, its empty cartridge cases, and all the clutter of his existence, it is part of the village landscape. Not for him the smart four by fours, their connectivity, their comfort. After all, what use is a mobile phone in the English countryside. Signal? What signal?

His concession to the C21 is, however, a battered laptop which gives him the email. He clearly finds this useful, although I do believe it is infrequently switched on. Nevertheless, it brought his world to a handful of his friends when I received, early one October morning, a truly wonderful message. I found it so moving that I quote it here, word for word. I hope you enjoy it as much as I did the day I received it. Once I had read it I said to myself "those are the words of a true, true countryman".

Sent at 07:18 on an early October morning it read as follows:

"I was woken this morning to incredible roaring and looked out of my bedroom window, which I can do just by turning over, and there about 30 yards away were two red deer stags challenging each other to a duel. Roaring, antlers clashing and thrashing about, all with the new sun starting to come up behind them. That upset all the geese and ducks on the other end of the potato field and they joined in protesting about it all until the noise was almost overwhelming. The stags have departed back to the wood after about 30 minutes of fighting and there are wave upon wave of wildfowl heading off to the marshes, most flying low over the house. The stags also upset two barn owls and a marsh harrier which are sitting on the top inside of the barn waiting for things to settle down.

I'm sitting here in the constant chorus of 'goose music' as they pour overhead, very low and into a head wind. Mallard, widgeon and teal are higher up in the sky and going faster. Looks like a couple of seals down on the mud too, filthy brutes will be eating my eels!

Stags have just reappeared (as I am writing this) chasing each other round the game mixture at the bottom of the garden".

Eggs in the kitchen after dark

EGGS

Any cook, whether starting to find their feet in the kitchen or striving for that third Michelin star, needs a plentiful supply of excellent eggs.

Enormous importance is attached to the humble, highly versatile, egg. The egg marks the very beginning for all cooks. Those who are using this book as a means to get started in cooking will probably know how to boil an egg. Those who know more will be arguing as to the best way to do it.

Whichever rung one has reached on the ladder of cooking capability one finds that eggs turn up everywhere. You may hopefully have your own chickens if you have the space, or perhaps you can be persuaded to keep a small number. I love my own chickens, ridiculous creatures though they may be, and I greatly value the ability to call on a supply of really fresh eggs whenever, almost, I need them.

Bantams are rather more fun and unquestionably prettier although Bantam cockerels can be more feisty than one might wish. I kept Bantams at one time and I did get a little tired of a particularly aggressive Sebright cockerel which took a very clear dislike to black Wellingtons. Fortunately the boots were thick enough to shield my ankles from his very sharp beak. Apart from this obvious disadvantage, bantam eggs are really rather small although otherwise similar to chicken eggs.

There is likely to be a farmers' market close to where you live, and many butchers sell good eggs. Never buy them from a supermarket – they cannot be truly fresh, no matter how they are described – unless, of course, the supermarket has a special arrangement with a very local supplier as one I know does. The complicated logistics of supermarket stocking make real freshness impossible. Due to the porosity of egg shells, total freshness cannot long be maintained and noticeable changes follow.

Four good laying chickens should produce around a couple of dozen eggs a week for the best part of the year. A breed of hens such as Rhode Island Red, Maran, Light Sussex or the hybrid Lehmann Brown will look after you well, although the Lehmanns in my experience do not seem to have a very long life span.

Chickens' eggs and ducks' eggs

Boiled

There are many ways of boiling eggs. You can put the egg in cold water and bring it to the boil; or plunge it into already boiling water; or put it into water at boiling point and then turn off the heat. The method I prefer for really fresh eggs, sometimes still warm from the lay, is to plunge them into water which is boiling in a lively manner and then to leave them there to boil for a good six minutes and then douse them in cold water as soon as you remove them from the heat. If you want a hard white but still some viscosity in the yolk leave them for about eight minutes. If you like them really hard at least nine minutes will be necessary. Over-boiling will make the yolk crumbly and create an unattractive grey ring between yolk and white when the egg is cut. Almost any Scotch egg you buy in any sandwich shop will demonstrate how it should not be done with a perfect grey ring! The freshness, size and temperature of the egg when it is immersed in the water will have a bearing on the precise boiling times, and it should be noted that I have been talking about very fresh eggs taken from the fridge.

Ducks' eggs can be treated like hens eggs, except that they may be more variable in size according to the breed and cooking times may have to be adjusted accordingly.

Poached

Poached eggs on toast is probably the most useful snack or light lunch ever devised. However, the eggs do need to be poached well to look attractive and this is not a pushover. The kitchens of very good hotels can easily produce dreadful looking poached eggs for breakfast. It is always a bad start to the day when your egg yolk has almost parted from the white, looking like a yellow balloon floating in a cirrus cloud.

A good method is to break the egg into a cup and then to slide the egg gently into a vortex of simmering water. This you achieve by boiling water in a saucepan, taking it off the heat so that the bubbling subsides, swirling the water round with a wooden spoon and sliding the egg into the whirlpool. All being well the egg will take on a perfect shape and the white will wrap neatly round the yolk. Then put the saucepan back on the heat and let it simmer quietly. The egg will be done in three to four minutes, depending upon how you like it. It helps to break the egg first into a cup and then slide it into the water, although if you feel more confident you can break the egg directly into the water but this does take a bit of practice and you have to be quick because the swirling will not last long. Poached eggs can be really wonderful with a wide array of dishes, so it is worthwhile perfecting the technique.

You can use an egg poacher which produces an acceptable result, but they are fiddly implements, awkward to clean and brilliant at scalding your fingers.

Scrambled

Heat up a small knob of butter in a pan so that the pan becomes well lubricated. Mix the yolks and whites together well with a fork and add them to the pan together with another small knob of butter and a splash of milk. Be careful not to apply too great a heat, and stir until you have the consistency you like. A little black pepper and a few fresh cut chives make a scrambled eggs look more attractive. They are better still with a little smoked salmon.

Omelettes

Making an omelette seems to be a very individual matter, but I shall set out how it works for me. It is important to develop a technique which hopefully works every time but it is unfortunately something that needs the cook's own experience before total confidence is reached. There is nothing inherently difficult about it, as is true of every recipe in this book. It is like riding a bicycle. Once mastered it is fairly difficult but far from impossible to fall off.

Steps to follow for an omelette for 2 people:

1. Use a **good solid frying pan**, spotlessly clean. **Oil it lightly**, both bottom and sides, with olive oil. Stainless steel is better than non-stick.

2. **Break** three eggs into a pudding basin and **add** a splash of cold water from the tap. **Beat** well with a fork, and then leave the mixture to settle for ten minutes.

3. **Heat** the oiled pan. **Pour** in the mixture. If the pan is sufficiently hot the mixture will sizzle as you pour.

4. **Maintain** a strong heat, and as the mixture starts to solidify keep it loose around the edges with a spatula.

5. Once the mixture is reasonably well set, **add** your filling of choice to that half of the pan nearest the handle and **spread** it evenly. Some fillings such as mushrooms or tomatoes will need to have been partly cooked in advance because they will not cook sufficiently in the short time before the omelette is ready.

6. Continue to let the mixture set but, before it sets completely, **turn** the half furthest from the pan handle over on top of the half on which you have spread the filling. **Turn down** the heat.

7. Leave the omelette, now semi-circular, to **cook a little further** but preferably leave the centre moist or even slightly runny or 'drizzling' as the French say. Now cut the semi-circle into two quadrants and serve.

Quails' eggs

That bright and lively little bird, the quail, produces tiny but delicious eggs. Many butchers sell both quails and their eggs. I once kept two quails of my own, until catastrophe struck. The quails lived in a moveable pen in an orchard and were happy there. Very sadly, a pair of Jack Russell terriers on the loose and out hunting as Jack Russells do, burrowed their way into the pen and totally consumed both birds. Not a feather was left. You can imagine my dismay on seeing that expression of satisfaction and pleasure on the dogs' faces when discovered, licking their lips while basking in the sun from behind the wire netting. It is true – Jack Russells really do smile!

To hard-boil quails' eggs plunge them into boiling water, maintain a lively heat for a good three minutes, and then plunge them into cold water. This prevents them from cooking further and seems to make them easier to peel.

You can try poaching them. A beautifully poached quails' egg placed on a bed of black olive tapenade, all on a tiny Italian biscuit, makes an impressive canapé. Breaking them whole properly is very tricky and it might be best left to the professionals!

VEGETABLES

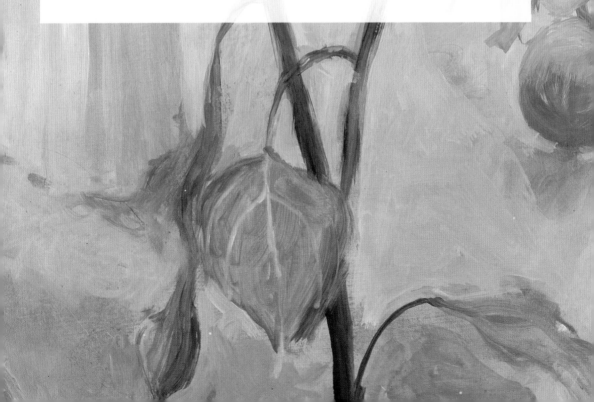

THE VEGETABLE RECIPES

Fashions in Britain for serving good vegetables seem to have waxed and waned over the past century or two, perhaps with the many social changes that have taken place over that time. In modern Britain the idea of 5-a-day in fruit and vegetables seems to have taken hold and here in Suffolk where excellent fruit and vegetables are grown to satisfy most needs we only miss some of the more exotic produce that is to be found in sunnier climes such as that of Provence. The choice of produce to accompany dishes is very much up to the cook, although some of my recipes do include suggestions for vegetables that I think go particularly well.

There are all kinds of vegetable suggestions, not only as accompaniments but as dishes in their own right. Asparagus, artichokes and aubergines feature amongst the recipes, as do tomatoes, onions, beetroot, peppers, leeks and others too. There are also recipes for ratatouille and salade Niçoise.

In contrast, this chapter has suggestions for roasting vegetables and making purées (which are especially delicious with game and Winter dishes) as well as guidance on the preparation of Provençal tomatoes and the use of tomatoes in salsa and salads.

What is vital is to have an understanding of the seasons if one is to avoid the wholly undesirable practice of buying vegetables from far flung corners of the globe, with the unnecessary cost involved and the hideous effect on the planet from carbon emissions. I always try to remember that it is not only aeroplanes that burn oil but ships too, reminding myself that there is no way out but to take full account of seasonality and buy from local sources.

This little matter of the seasons was brought home to me vividly one February day at a market gardener's fruit and vegetable stall which supplies one of our East Suffolk market towns with flowers, fruit and vegetables twice a week all through the year.

Picture the scene in this historic place, where trade has continued more or less uninterrupted since the C13 – the cold wind whistling around the market, any conversation drowned by the noise of the flapping blue and white canvas covering the stalls. The biting Easterly chills the small queue of regulars who survey the vegetables on offer and reflect on the choices they will make. The vegetables are mostly home grown – celeriac, turnips, parsnips, cauliflower, swedes, cabbages, sweet potatoes...

Suddenly, at the back of the queue a tall, well dressed man shouts out:

"Have you got any mange-tout?" The stallholder politely replies that they are out of season.

"Have you got peas?" comes the riposte.

"Sorry, they're out of season too."

The people in the queue turn their heads in unison towards the stranger, as if commanded by a hidden power. The man consults his shopping list and shouts against the wind.

"Some courgettes then."

"No, out of season." comes the somewhat peremptory reply.

The stallholder, rapidly losing interest, starts to tidy up his oranges and knock the hard earth off the celeriac and clean up the beetroot. The stranger shouts again.

"What about French beans?"

"Out of season – next please" shouts the stallholder, not even bothering to look up. The stranger hesitates for a moment, his face reddening despite the biting wind. He consults his list again and turns away. Game, set and match to the stallholder!

Cabbage Whites

COOKING GUIDELINES FOR VEGETABLES

Vegetables vary enormously in size, maturity and freshness, and all these factors affect cooking times. The indications given below can be no more than guidelines, especially as tastes vary enormously as to whether vegetables should be well cooked or crunchily al dente.

The two principal methods are **boiling and steaming**. Whereas the time honoured and traditional method is by boiling, steaming preserves the nutrients in vegetables admirably. I have to admit that **the ease of steaming** as well as its benefits attracts me more and more, and I now find myself naturally reaching for the steamer instead of boiling the kettle. Not only does a steamer produce excellent cooked vegetables, the arrangement of the steamer in tiers makes it much easier to bring everything together at the right moment.

However, I did find on my journey along the cookery road that it would have been extremely useful to have had, ready to hand, timing guidelines for boiling vegetables. These guidelines also give a good idea as to how long steaming will take.

The boiling times given assume that the boiling water will be **bubbling in a lively manner at the moment the vegetable is plunged in**, unless otherwise stated. Similarly, steaming times relate to a steamer which is already boiling and **not** to a steamer which has just been put on the heat.

Included with these basic instructions are a few short recipes in which certain vegetables can be attractively cooked to increase their appeal.

In addition I have explained an absolutely invaluable technique for peeling tomatoes.

Guidelines

Beetroot
Do not trim or peel the beetroot as it will bleed severely in the boiling water. The timing will be heavily dependent on the size of the individual beetroot. A small one might cook in 30 minutes or less whereas a large root may take 90 minutes. Ensure that the saucepan does not boil dry. (I have not improved a number of saucepans this way...). When you think that they are cooked, test them with a sharp pointed knife.

Beans

Broad: boil for about 10–12 minutes according to size and age.

Runner: trim ends, de-string them and boil for 12–15 minutes.

French: trim ends and boil for about 8 minutes.

Dried: butter beans, cannelloni beans, flageolet beans and kidney beans all need to be soaked overnight in cold water. This helps to reduce indigestible compounds. They then need to be boiled until soft which can take between one and two hours.

Broccoli (Calabrese)

Cut off the stalks, separate the florets and boil for about 5 minutes.

Brussels sprouts

Peel off the outer leaves and cut a cross in the base. This ensures they will cook through. Plunge them into boiling water and boil for about 12 minutes. If left too long they will produce a smell worthy of the very worst institutional food.

Butternut squash

Roast for at least 60 minutes.

Cabbage

Cut into smallish pieces and boil for 10 minutes. 12–14 minutes for Red Cabbage.

Carrots

Sizeable carrots take a long time: if cut into short lengths boil for 20 minutes. They might otherwise take a good 30 minutes. In a slow cooked stew they can take hours. A Frenchman I know from Aix makes an excellent rabbit stew which takes about three hours. He says that once the carrots are done the stew is ready.

Cauliflower

Can be the dullest of vegetables unless made into a purée. Cut off the florets and discard the stalk, and plunge them into boiling water and boil for 10–12 minutes. Remove from the heat, drain them and put them in a ready warmed bowl with a good knob of butter, perhaps 25g or so. Purée with a blender. The result is almost moreish! Cauliflower also roasts well★.

Celeriac

Cut off all the rough skin, dice the celeriac into 20mm lumps and boil for about 30 minutes or until a sharp pointed knife can be inserted with ease. It can be mashed like potato with milk and butter. Turn it into a mousseline★ for maximum enjoyment.

★ *Roast cauliflower, p.197, 198; Mousseline, p.195*

Courgettes
Boil for 6 to 8 minutes.

Chard
Boil for 5 minutes.

Kale
Cut off the stalks and boil for 8 minutes.

Leeks
Trim the ends, making sure all the soil has been washed out from between the leaves. Cut into short lengths and boil for 9 minutes. Drain well.

Lentils
Puy variety, dried: rinse the lentils in cold water and cover them with double the volume of water as lentils. Do not add salt. Bring to a simmer and cook until tender which will take about 20 minutes.

Split red variety: these do not retain their shape in the cooking like Puy lentils. They also require a much shorter cooking time. About 7 minutes is enough.

Mangetout (sugar snap peas)
They need to be crisp, so boil for 2–4 minutes.

Onions
Saute quarters gently in oil until soft or boil whole for 15 minutes.

Parsnips
Peel and core, and cut each parsnip into three or four pieces and boil for 20 minutes. They are excellent roasted*.

Peas
If frozen, boil for 3 minutes If fresh boil for 4–5 minutes.

Potatoes
For mashing or for a purée: dice into small lumps of around 10mm and boil for about 20 minutes or until soft and easy to mash, or blend into a purée or mousseline.

For a saute: parboil in the size you need for the plate until they are reasonably soft. Test them with a pointed knife. Then put them in a frying pan with a little olive oil and garlic (and perhaps some fresh rosemary) and fry them gently for 20 minutes, turning them frequently.

---

* *Roast winter vegetables, p.197*

For boiling: boil for about 25 minutes according to size, including unpeeled new potatoes.

For roasting: parboil for at least 15 minutes and drain. Throw them from colander to saucepan, and saucepan to colander, to rough up the edges a little. Now put them in a roasting tray on their own with olive oil, garlic and rosemary and roast for at least 50 minutes in a hot oven. For a less healthy alternative put them in the roasting tray if you are cooking beef. You may wish to avoid putting them with poultry, lamb or pork as they soak up so much fat. Turn them occasionally.

For baking in their skins: the old farm workers' trick of putting them in the ash of a bonfire for an hour or so works well, but if you do not happen to have a hot bonfire to hand they will cook in a hot oven in about 75 minutes depending on size.

Purple and white sprouting broccoli
Cut off all the stalks and boil the new shoots for about 5 minutes.

Turnips
Peel and dice into lumps, and boil for about 12 minutes, Drain and swill them round with a knob of butter in the hot saucepan you have used to boil them.

Samphire
It just needs to be warmed gently with butter, but remember to wash off the salt very thoroughly beforehand.

Spinach
Wash the leaves and leave them really wet, and put them in a lidded saucepan with 1cm of water. Boil for 3 to 4 minutes, or until the wet leaves collapse into the bottom of the saucepan. Baby spinach leaves need less time.

Swede
Dice into smallish lumps and boil for 20 minutes.

Sweet potatoes
Bake whole for about 60 minutes at Gas 5, 190C, or if diced, boil for about 20 minutes.

LENTIL STEW

Highly nourishing, lentils have been a staple food for centuries in Asia and Europe and deserve to be more popular than they seem to be at the present time. They are most warming and comforting and the following easy recipe enables them to be matched with a wide variety of foods, traditionally with pork but also with poultry and game birds.

Ingredients (Serves 2)
250g of Puy lentils, (ready to eat)
2 carrots, sliced
1 tomato, chopped
4 garlic cloves, crushed
3 tablespoons of olive oil
1 ½ glasses of red wine or port
2 small shallots, finely chopped
seasoning

Preheat the oven to Gas 2, 150C.

Boil the sliced carrots until soft. **Fry** the chopped shallots very gently in olive oil. **Combine** all the ingredients together, season and cook for 45 minutes.

POTATO AND CELERIAC IN THE STYLE OF A MOUSSELINE

This is a really wonderful accompaniment to game, especially to venison, but it also makes an ideal winter accompaniment to all red meats.

A purée can be prepared simply with mashed potato and mashed celeriac alone. However, the real delight is to make it in the style of a mousseline. This is done by adding some fat free Greek yoghurt (a true mousseline contains whipped cream) to the potato and celeriac after they have been combined together.

The key is to make a mashed potato of super smoothness, and this means that the time honoured English fashion of pounding away with a hand held masher needs to be abandoned in favour of a blender.

Ingredients (Serves 2)
200g of potato, after having been peeled
300g of celeriac, after having been peeled
a little milk, warmed
a knob of butter, softened
1 tablespoon of fat free Greek yoghurt

Dice the potato and **boil** until soft. **Separately**, dice the celeriac and **boil** until soft. **Add** a little warmed milk to the potatoes and a knob of softened butter and **blend** until really smooth. The blending will be achieved very quickly.

Now **add** a knob of softened butter to the celeriac and **blend** until smooth, although do not expect it to become as a smooth as the potato.

Now **merge** the potato and celeriac together and stir well, at the same time stirring in the yoghurt. Do not exceed one tablespoon.

Before serving, **warm gently** to reach the desired temperature.

· · · · · · · · · ·

Lemon mashed potatoes

Where conventional hand-mashed potatoes are preferred, the addition of lemon zest is attractive. **Boil** the potatoes (500g) together with two bay leaves, until soft. Discard the bay leaves and **add** 50ml of milk, a knob of butter, 2 tablespoons of olive oil and the **very finely grated** zest of 1 lemon. Warm up and mash in the usual way.

CARROT PURÉE

Oh so simple! The easiest recipe in this book. Have I said that before? It is still worthwhile putting it in your repertoire because the humble carrot needs something to cheer it up, otherwise it is for the horses. It is of course good for you and packed with vitamin C. The purée is good with roast meats and game and looks rather impressive if presented on a plate decorated with florets of Romanesco cauliflower!

Ingredients (Serves 2)
250g of carrots, after having been peeled
a knob of butter, softened
1 dessertspoon of fat free Greek yoghurt
a pinch of black pepper

Slice the peeled carrot into rings and boil until soft. Carrots are notoriously slow to cook, and much depends on the thickness of the rings. A rough estimate is that they will be soft in around 25 minutes.

Add the knob of softened butter to the carrots and the pepper, **Blend** until smooth. Stir in one dessertspoonful – not more – of yoghurt.

Before serving heat gently to bring up to the desired temperature.

ROAST WINTER VEGETABLES

This a very attractive way of serving a variety of vegetables and a method of adding to the appeal of many a winter roast of meat or game. It is especially suited to root vegetables but when certain green vegetables are added the visual appeal is improved as well as the taste. It is suitable for:

> beetroot (parboil first)
> broccoli (both calabrese and purple sprouting)
> carrots (peeled)
> cauliflower (floret)
> garlic (peeled)
> leeks (trim, clean and cut into short lengths)
> parsnips (peel, and remove any core)
> onions, red or white (skin and quarter)
> shallots (skinned)
> swede (skinned)
> tomatoes (halved)
> turnips (peeled)

Choose your vegetables, **prepare** as necessary and **cut** them into bite-sized chunks. The cooking time will relate to the size of the chunks. **Stir** them around in a large bowl with a generous helping of olive oil and dried English herbs. It is important also to **add** fresh rosemary sprigs and two or three bay leaves. **Stir** again and **leave** for at least an hour.

Preheat the oven to Gas 6, 200C.

Stir the vegetables again and **add** a little more olive oil if necessary. **Transfer** them to a baking tray and spread them out. **Roast** for a good hour, which is about right for bite sized chunks.

ROAST CAULIFLOWER AND CALABRESE

Where an all green addition is needed, this makes an attractive combination. The method is very similar to that for roasting winter vegetables but as root vegetables are not included it is a little quicker to do.

Ingredients (Serves 4)
12 florets of cauliflower
12 florets of Romanesco cauliflower
12 florets of calabrese
2 tablespoons of olive oil
2 garlic cloves, crushed
dried English herbs

Preheat the oven to Gas 6, 200C.

Stir the crushed garlic around in olive oil and leave to **infuse** for a few minutes.

Remove the florets neatly from their respective stalks, put them in a large bowl and **sprinkle** all the olive oil over them. **Add** the dried herbs or alternatively use chopped fresh herbs if you have them. Coriander, dill and fennel go well.

Now **stir** it all about so that the vegetables are all coated with the flavoured oil and leave for 30 minutes or so.

Arrange the vegetables in a roasting tray sufficiently large to ensure the florets are not on top of each other, and **roast** for 30 minutes or so, **turning** them all after 15 minutes to distribute the heat.

The calabrese is always very delicious if a little scorched, so do not worry if it looks a bit blackened at the finish.

Between the beans

TOMATOES

Although tomatoes are botanically classified as fruits from the nightshade family, their role as a fruit-cum-vegetable is so indispensable to the cook that they are included without apology in the vegetable section of this book.

Native to South America, the tomato was imported into Spain in the C16 and crept Northwards over the next 200 years, although doubtless established itself as a vital element in the cooking of Provence and other Mediterranean regions very quickly.

Tomatoes are, of course, produced in huge quantities in the Mediterranean countries although the cook in Aldeburgh has almost as much need for them as the cook in Aix-en-Provence. Suffolk tomatoes may, however, not look quite the same as the Marmandes (which in Britain are known as beef tomatoes) grown in Provence, but that is not important. Their wondrous qualities of being low in calories, yet high in vitamins A, B and C (as well as being somewhat laxative and diuretic) are only offset by their acidity and indigestible skins, which brings us to the very important matter of peeling them.

Peeling tomatoes

Many recipes are much improved if the tomatoes are peeled, and at first sight this is near impossible to achieve neatly. The following technique will save hours of heartache.

1. Cover the tomatoes in cold water and heat them gently.

2. When the water is hot the skins will have softened and will start to crack.

3. As soon as the skins begin to split remove the tomatoes from the heat and place them on a chopping board.

4. Cut them in half through the stalk and place each half flat side down on the board.

5. Pinch the skin between thumb and forefinger and the entire half-skin will detach cleanly, leaving the flesh of the tomato itself more or less untouched.

TOMATO RECIPES

Tomato Salsa

Now that the peeling of tomatoes is no longer a mystery it is well worthwhile making tomato salsa which is a delicious and refreshing accompaniment to many summer dishes. Not all recipes call for peeled tomatoes although many do, but the decision can often be taken according to the state of the tomato skins and how soft they are, or whether or not you dislike eating the raw skins. The crunchiness of tomatoes which remain with their skins has some appeal, but those which have been skinned and then diced make a smoother and more elegant accompaniment to what might be a most distinguished fish, such as a poached wild sea trout for which this salsa is ideal.

> 500g of tomatoes, peeled and diced very finely
> 2 small red onions, diced very finely
> 1 tablespoon of top quality red wine vinegar
> 1 teaspoon of caster sugar

Peel the onions and **dice** them into **tiny cubes**. Peel the tomatoes if you wish, and dice them **also into tiny cubes**, although if they are not peeled they will dice more easily. You will find a hand held dicer very effective for this task which is otherwise difficult and labour intensive. **Add** the sugar and the vinegar and mix well with a spoon.

It is important that the ingredients marry well. The finished salsa will benefit considerably from being in the fridge for four hours or even longer. Serve cold. This recipe will be sufficient for four.

Tomato salad

This may be thought to be so simple that it is all obvious. However, it is worthwhile slicing the tomatoes thinly, and laying the slices individually on a plate, sprinkling them with black pepper and then **decorating** them with chopped fresh herbs such as basil or tarragon. If none is available decorate with parsley, flat or crinkly. About **an hour before serving** drizzle the salad with olive oil, sprinkle it with sea salt and put it in the fridge. It can sometimes look attractive if decorated with a few white flowers, but leave this until the last minute.

Tomatoes à la Provençale

Preheat the oven to Gas 6, 200C.

Tomatoes prepared and cooked in the Provençal manner are immensely useful. There are several methods frequently used but this simple recipe will always add an interesting feature to a wide variety of fish and meat dishes.

For two people cut the top off two large, ripe tomatoes. (If you are using beef tomatoes one tomato cut in half is sufficient for two people). Shred four garlic cloves and mix in a little dried thyme or a very small pinch of herbs of Provence. Make incisions in the flesh and gently press the garlic and herbal mixture into each half. At that point season with a little salt and black pepper. Then sprinkle white breadcrumbs mixed with a little chopped parsley on top, and drizzle with olive oil.

Roast in an oiled tray for about 45 minutes at Gas 6, 200C, or until the breadcrumbs start to brown.

Cherry tomatoes in a Provençale style

If possible, seek out cherry tomatoes of varying colours – red, orange, yellow, purple – which are so moreish when raw that they tend to disappear like Smarties. However, they make a light and refreshing first course when very slow cooked, or when used as a simple accompaniment to a fish. Try them with a baked freshwater trout. Cooked in this way they are a variation of the well known recipe for Tomatoes à la Provençale (above) which is an attribute to so many Mediterranean dishes.

Take eight cherry tomatoes per person and cut them in half through the stalks. Lay them on an oiled baking tray and season with a little salt. Now shred two garlic cloves per person and put a few shreds on each half-tomato. Then drizzle some olive oil over the tomatoes and finish by sprinkling them with dried thyme or herbs of Provence.

Slow bake in a very cool oven for at least two hours.

SAUCES

Savoury

Sweet

THE SAUCE RECIPES

Not so long ago, I was terrified by sauces. How on earth could one create such smooth, sophisticated accompaniments? Equally terrified of the word 'gravy' for entirely different reasons (shades of institutional catering I think) the food I cooked tended to be somewhat dry. Making a sauce was the sound barrier to the stratospheric world of real cooking. It was evidently complicated, time consuming and expensive, and surrounded in mystique.

The other side of the 'terror' coin was horror, and the horror was because of some of the lacklustre sauces we see so often, which when analysed are not much more than dull old brown or equally dull old white sauces dressed up one way or another and named for appeal.

I must say I wondered how to start in this frightening new world until one rainy day in Shropshire, where it always rains or threatens to, when I came across a newspaper feature which described such a sensible sauce for game that I just had to try out. It suddenly struck me that making sauces might actually be possible for mere mortals. What I needed was a little confidence.

My first attempt was a disaster, but there seems to be an explanation – being in too much of a hurry. When the recipe says, for example, add flour little by little, or slowly, or gradually, it means what it says. So say to yourself – that's too fast – so slow it down. Then halve the speed again.

This chapter contains a variety of easy sauces to get you started. They are simple to prepare and do not require any special techniques although aïoli sauce, which is the very essence of Provence, will need practice. Aïoli sauce is a garlic mayonnaise used to complement many everyday dishes in Provence and also gives its name to two traditional dishes in their own right.

Aïoli sauce is a vital element in *bourride*, a fish stew which is one of the great dishes of Provence, usually made from monkfish and bound together with the aïoli. An *aïoli garni* is a medley of vegetables such as potatoes, carrots, beans and other green vegetables in season together with fish, possibly salt cod, and perhaps some cooked snails, whereas the ultimate variation, a *grand aïoli*, will have meats added too. However, I have not attempted to venture into these territories and if you succeed in making aïoli sauce alone you should feel well pleased.

AÏOLI

Aïoli is the very life blood of Provençal cooking. It is that deliciously smooth garlic mayonnaise that happily accompanies so many foods – probably potato above all others – and which gives its name to *aïoli garni* and *grand aïoli* mentioned earlier. However, this recipe is for the mayonnaise alone.

Aïoli is a wonderful companion to any kind of salad you might feel like making and is well worth the patience and rather hard work required to create it. However, the method is extremely simple and you should not shy away from making it as I have to confess I did for a very long time, but it is a bit like riding a bicycle – easy when you have had a bit of practice.

Ingredients (Sufficient for 4)
4 or 5 large garlic cloves, peeled and crushed
150 ml or so of olive oil (from Provence if possible)
2 egg yolks
a pinch of salt
¼ of a small lemon, squeezed

Crush the garlic to pulp in a garlic press, and then pulp it further, preferably in a pestle and mortar or otherwise with a wooden spoon in a bowl.

Add the egg yolks to the garlic together with a pinch of salt and stir very well with a wooden spoon so that these ingredients are well and truly mixed.

Now **start to add** the olive oil **literally drop by drop**, mixing the drops in with the wooden spoon and **stirring continually**. **Do not stop stirring!**

After a time the aïoli will begin to thicken and then it will be possible to increase the speed of adding the drops. As it thickens further a trickle (**but keep stirring**) will thicken the aïoli even more. When it is really quite thick mix in the lemon juice. **Always keep aïoli refrigerated**.

If it goes wrong and curdles because the drops have been added too fast, add the curdled mixture slowly to another yolk in a clean bowl. This should save the day.

An electric mixer, **carefully used**, saves time and arm-ache.

ANCHOVY SAUCE

This sauce is most useful for accompanying different sorts of white fish, especially the rather more meaty fish such as cod or haddock. I particularly like it with roast haddock fillet*, lemon mashed potatoes* and Provençal tomatoes*. It is a favourite in my household.

Ingredients (Sufficient for 4)
50g anchovy fillets (tinned anchovies in olive oil), crushed
20g butter
2 large garlic cloves, crushed
a few drops of olive oil
1 dessertspoon of tomato purée
2 dessertspoons of inexpensive Cognac

Wash and dry the anchovies. **Crush** the garlic cloves into the anchovies using a pestle and mortar if you have one (otherwise ensure that the anchovies and garlic are crushed to a paste with a wooden spoon) and then transfer them to a small saucepan.

Add the butter and mix together, warming gently. **Add** the tomato purée and when these ingredients have nicely combined together **add** the Cognac and **stir** well.

---

* *Haddock with anchovy sauce, p.108; Lemon mashed potatoes, p.195; Tomatoes à la Provençale, p.202*

CAPER SAUCE

Capers are the buds of the *Capparis spinosa*, a flowering shrub prevalent in Southern Europe, although the buds of the nasturtium are sometimes used as a substitute. Used as flavouring since Roman times, capers provide a tangy contrast for various fishes. This simple sauce is an excellent complement to skate. As capers are normally preserved in vinegar or salt, they always need to be very well washed in running water.

There are various methods of making the sauce but I use the simplest possible method combining them with butter and black pepper.

Ingredients (Serves 2)
2 tablespoons of capers, very well washed
30g of butter
black pepper

Melt the butter in a saucepan so that it becomes liquid, but **do not** heat it so that it burns or becomes clarified.

Immerse the capers in the butter **adding** black pepper from the pepper mill to taste. **Stir** and maintain a gentle heat until required.

COURGETTE AND TOMATO SAUCE

Courgettes and tomatoes are excellent partners whether as vegetables to accompany fish or meat, as a first course or as a sauce. This recipe is halfway between an accompanying vegetable and a sauce, and has been designed to complement white fish. It is especially useful for filleted Dover and Lemon sole and plaice, and is good with monkfish tail.

> **Ingredients (Sufficient for 2)**
> 450ml of fish stock, reduced to 100ml
> 1 medium size courgette, cut into matchsticks
> 2 medium size and firm tomatoes, peeled and diced
> fresh parsley, chopped
> a knob of butter

Prepare the fish stock from good quality fish stock cubes, unless you have taken the purist line and made your fish stock from turbot bones! **Dissolve** the cubes thoroughly and then boil the stock so as to **reduce** it to about 100 ml of concentrate. This will take a little time but beware of reducing it too much. It can swiftly boil away to nothing at the end if you do not keep a careful watch on it, although at the start it is easy to become impatient as nothing seems to be happening. This operation can be done in advance and the stock refrigerated.

Peel the tomatoes★ and when cool dice them into very small pieces.

Slice the courgettes into matchsticks. This is easy once you develop your own cutting technique. Now **fry** the courgettes gently in a little olive oil for about a minute in a frying pan.

Then **add** the diced tomatoes to the courgettes in the frying pan together with a knob of butter and **fry** the courgettes and tomatoes gently for two to three minutes.

Now **add** the courgettes and tomatoes to the stock with all their cooking juices. **Stir** well together with some freshly chopped parsley. Serve with the fish.

★ *Peeling tomatoes, p.200*

MADEIRA SAUCE

Madeira, that once ever so fashionable wine found in every prosperous household in England, is the perfect wine for making sauce. Unlike other wines it is no stranger to heat, as it is heated considerably during its production. Perhaps that accounts for the fact that it is a natural ingredient for sauce, but it always retains that little tang which makes it so attractive.

I much prefer the traditional way of making Madeira sauce which meant adding the wine to reduced meat stock, rather than the complex modern methods that are more fashionable.

The method I have devised will suit meat, game or poultry depending on the stock used.

Ingredients
200 ml of meat stock, or chicken stock
150ml of sweet Madeira
1 tablespoon of redcurrant jelly
black pepper

Prepare a strong solution of the stock.

For meat or game use meat stock and **reduce** it over a lively heat down to 100ml. For chicken use chicken stock in the same way.

Let it **reduce quite quickly**. Once it has reduced by about a quarter stir in the tablespoon of redcurrant jelly.

Now **add** the Madeira and a little ground black pepper. **Reduce** the whole solution down to about 100ml or the volume you require. The greater the reduction the more intense the flavours will become.

PROVENÇALE SAUCE

Provençal sauce describes a multitude of preparations which have the Provençal characteristics. Certain ingredients invariably predominate as in most things Provençal, notably olive oil, tomato and garlic, all three of which run through then like a rich vein of Mediterranean sunshine. The sauce is especially useful for accompanying fish, poultry, vegetables and eggs. It often includes mushrooms and is frequently expanded by the addition of onions, aubergines, black or green olives and white wine. Herbs, too, are nearly always included and lemon juice often adds to its savours.

Dishes in this book which are described as Provençal or à la Provençale will have incorporated a sauce in this style, although countless recipes for a sauce of this kind exist. They will have been developed over thousands of lifetimes of cooking and will embody the flair and creativeness of their individual cooks.

The following is an example of how it might be done.

Ingredients
3 tablespoons of olive oil
3 tablespoons of onions or shallots, finely chopped
750g of tomatoes, peeled and chopped
2 garlic cloves, crushed
a splash of white wine from Provence
herbs of Provence
fresh parsley and basil, chopped

Peel the tomatoes★ and **chop** them well. **Warm** the olive oil a little, and **cook** the onions, with the garlic, **very gently** for about 10 minutes so that they soften and discolour. **On no account let them brown** or burn. Then **add** the tomatoes, the splash of wine and the herbs and let it all stew together for about 15 minutes. Allow further time for it to **reduce** so that it **thickens** to the consistency you need. **Add** some chopped parsley and basil before serving.

★ *Peeling tomatoes, p.200*

RED WINE SAUCE FOR GAME AND BEEF

This sauce is particularly suitable for game and especially good with partridge, but is also admirable with pheasant and venison all of which take naturally to a robust red wine and to redcurrant jelly. They also take wonderfully well to quince and apple jelly which I discovered quite by chance when the redcurrant jelly ran out.

Ingredients

for game
150ml of red wine
1 heaped tablespoonful of redcurrant jelly (or quince and apple jelly)
200 ml of meat stock, to be reduced to about 150ml
ground black pepper to taste

for a peppery sauce for beef
include the red wine and the meat stock, plus
1 teaspoonful of redcurrant jelly
whole black peppercorns and more ground pepper

For both game and beef prepare a **strong** solution of meat stock and place it on a lively heat so that it starts to **reduce** quite quickly. Once it has reduced by about a quarter stir in the redcurrant jelly: **a heaped tablespoon for game** and **a teaspoon for beef**.

Now **add** the red wine, and **reduce** the solution over a lively heat until you have roughly 100ml, or the quantity you need. **For game or beef add** ground pepper as you wish. **For beef alone add** whole black peppercorns as well.

The more the liquid boils the more it will reduce and the more intense in flavour it will become, but be careful not to let it boil away to nothing which it can do surprisingly quickly.

You may well want to adjust the quantities of the ingredients to suit your taste and requirements. **Experiment** with the quantities, and the reduction process, until experience tells you how you like to have the sauce.

TOMATO SAUCE

Tomato sauce! What horrors do those two words conjure up for the British! Shades of the roadside diner, the odours of diesel and hot engines permeating the room on a summer's day. Or perhaps the grease laden atmosphere impregnating one's clothes as the rain lashes the windows in winter!

In fact a real tomato sauce is a most useful and nutritious creation and is very much a feature of Provençal cooking and the Provençal diet. The wonderful choice of fruit and vegetables to be found in Provence gives a choice of tomato varieties too, and the Provençal preference is for a tomato variety known as St Pierre.

A genuine tomato sauce, (perhaps more accurately called a tomato coulis) may be cold or hot, both versions retaining intact the tomato's exceptional store of vitamins and nutrients.

For a cold coulis: Peel★ 5 large tomatoes. **Crush** them using a pestle and mortar if you have one, otherwise use a pudding bowl and a wooden spoon. **Crush** 4 fat garlic cloves and **mix** them into the tomatoes, making a juicy mixture. **Add** the juice of half a lemon. Now **add** a few drops of olive oil. Salt the mixture very lightly, **mix** well by hand and ensure the ingredients have properly blended.

For a hot sauce: Peel★ and crush 1 kilo of tomatoes. Chop up 200g of onions. Crush 3 garlic cloves and chop up some parsley. Mix the garlic and parsley together.

Heat the onions in olive oil until they discolour, but do not let them brown. Then **add** the tomatoes and the garlic / parsley mixture. **Cook** over a low heat for a few minutes, stirring all the time.

Now **add** half a teaspoonful of caster sugar, a bay leaf, some fresh basil, and some (preferably fresh) thyme. Season and **stir well**. **Simmer** gently for at least 45 minutes over a low heat. When cooked, remove the bay leaf and **add** some freshly cut basil and **stir**.

★ *Peeling tomatoes, p.200*

WHITE WINE SAUCE FOR FISH

For those of us who have taught ourselves to cook, gleaning whatever we could on the long journey from the cool air of Suffolk where the Romans used to have their own white wine vineyards to the sun soaked vines of Provence, we are inclined to think that wine based sauces are rather complicated. Doubtless they can be, but keeping it simple is one of the mantras of this book. The following recipe makes an excellent accompaniment for many different kinds of white fish.

Ingredients
150 ml of white wine (or alternatively Aspall's Suffolk cyder)
150 ml of fish stock (1 stock cube is sufficient)
1 egg yolk
10g of butter

Prepare the stock using one organic (and preferably low salt) fish stock cube and bring it to the boil. **Allow** it to continue boiling over a lively heat for three or four minutes, by which time it will have reduced to some extent.

Now **add** the white wine and bring to the **boil again**, letting the boiling continue so that the volume of liquid is substantially reduced. Then **remove** it from the heat and let it cool for several minutes.

Separate very carefully the egg white from the yolk and put the white aside for another use. Then **break** into the yolk with a fork so that it runs and **stir** it in **little by little** to thicken the sauce. Do this over an extremely gentle heat.

Finally **add** the butter, again little by little, and still over the very gentle heat, **stir** continuously.

The sauce is ideal for many simply cooked white fish.

Under the apples

APPLE SAUCE

This is, of course, the classic accompaniment to roast pork but is also good with duck or goose as it is the kind of sauce which attenuates the richness of certain foods. Pork with apple sauce is traditionally English – very Suffolk too.

Nevertheless, a delicious roast loin of pork with crunchy crackling and plentiful apple sauce might take your imagination to a Suffolk orchard basking in the summer sunshine, its peacefulness punctuated periodically by a snort or two from a perspiring pig and the sound of a chuntering goose as the Bramley apples silently ripen on their trees. Have I been carried away into the depths of rural Suffolk? After all, apple sauce is only apple sauce! But it is well worthwhile and simple to prepare.

Ingredients (Serves 4)
500g of Bramley apples, peeled, cored and roughly chopped
15g of butter
half a lemon, squeezed
4 strips of lemon zest
2 tablespoons of water
caster sugar to taste

Core, **peel and chop** the apples. **Slice** off thin strips of lemon zest. Pour the water into a pan making sure that there is sufficient to cover the bottom. Start to warm the pan gently, and **add** the lemon zest and butter. Now **add** the apples and **stew** gently until the apples are soft. They will soften quite quickly.

Now **beat** the stew to a smooth paste, **strain** off any excess liquid, and then **rub** through a sieve. **Reheat** gently, **stirring** in the lemon juice, and sweeten to your taste.

BULLACE SAUCE

The bullace is a semi–wild plum which I always think of as being very 'Suffolk' although it does appear in other parts of Britain The bullace tree is not, however, widely known. It is a subspecies of the domestic plum, mostly producing a plum coloured fruit. A closely related but less common variety is the Shepherd's Bullace which I just happen to have in my garden. It has sharp, acidic little plum shaped fruits which do not ripen until November when they take on a pinky-yellow hue.

The reader may well be wondering why I am wasting their time with the bullace. The answer is that it makes heavenly sauce which is perfect with wild duck. As both wild duck and bullaces are at their best at the same time of year it would be a pity to ignore them.

So as and when you get the chance, seize it. The duck and the sauce will remain in your memory and you will search both out the following year.

To make the sauce, follow precisely the instructions for gooseberry sauce⋆ in this book.

⋆ *Gooseberry sauce, p.218*

CHOCOLATE SAUCE

There are seemingly endless recipes for chocolate sauce and everyone you ask will have a different idea, many of them being unnecessarily complicated. The recipe I propose is simplicity itself and will produce a smooth, glossy sauce.

When making anything in chocolate use the very best plain chocolate you can find. Depending upon the degree of sweetness you like there are a number of really delicious chocolate bars available from different makers containing 70% or more of cocoa solids. I always enjoy Valrhona, Menier by Nestle, or Lindt 85%. The sugar content of each varies, and so your own sweetness requirement is the deciding factor. My own preference is for the higher percentage products.

Ingredients (Sufficient for 2+)
100g bar of plain chocolate (minimum 70% cocoa solids) well broken up
30g of butter, diced into small lumps
100 ml of water

Warm the chocolate and water together in a heavy pan over a low heat, **stirring** all the time until the mixture is smooth.

Then **remove** the pan from the heat and **stir** in a few lumps of butter, **adding more and stirring** as they melt. Once all the butter has been incorporated into the chocolate give the sauce a **final stir** and serve.

GOOSEBERRY SAUCE

The taste of gooseberries with mackerel is one of those traditions which always comes as a surprise, and a delightful surprise it is. The two are firmly linked together in the French word for gooseberry which also seems a bit of a surprise in itself. But there it is – *groseille a maquereau.*

This sauce is wonderful with smoked mackerel★, and good with fresh mackerel too. As a light supper dish hot-smoked mackerel served cold with gooseberry sauce is difficult to beat.

Ingredients (Serves 4)
250g of gooseberries, topped and tailed
100ml water
10g of butter
20g of Demerera sugar (or more or less as you wish)
half a smallish lemon, squeezed

Top and tail the gooseberries. This takes a few minutes. Try to find, or grow, the sweeter red varieties. Green gooseberries are so very, very green, and need a great deal of sugar.

Gently stew the gooseberries in the water until pulpy together with the butter. Stewing happens very quickly. Then **beat the pulp** with a wooden spoon and press very firmly through a **sieve** to produce a smooth sauce without skins and pips. **Reheat** the sauce, **stir** in the sugar, and then the lemon juice.

If the sauce is too runny, keep it on a moderate heat to reduce it so that it thickens. Refrigerate.

Stick to the quantities apart from the sugar weight which can be adjusted according to the sweetness of the gooseberries and your own taste.

Note: this method is equally suitable for a bullace or plum sauce.

★ *Smoked mackerel, p.92*

ORANGE SAUCE

This sauce is ideal for roast duck or guinea fowl and simple to prepare. It is a subtle alternative to the sauce or gravy which is so often served with duck. I created the sauce from ingredients which were ready to hand in my kitchen and while I cannot claim that it has much to do with Suffolk or Provence I am sure the influences of both regions are there.

Ingredients (Sufficient for 4)
200 ml of meat stock, before reduction (see below)
1 orange, juice and zest
a handful of black peppercorns
1 dessertspoon of redcurrant jelly
a splash of fino sherry

Prepare 200 ml of meat stock from two beef stock tablets and **reduce** it to about 100ml by boiling it over a lively heat.

Strip three or four long lengths of zest from the orange, and then squeeze the orange.

Put the juice in another pan together with the strips of zest. **Heat** the juice and zest and simmer gently for a while, letting the juice reduce a little.

Now **add** the orange juice and zest to the reduced meat stock, together with the peppercorns. Then **add** the redcurrant jelly keeping the sauce hot and stirring well so that the jelly melts. Finally, **add** a splash of very dry (fino) sherry.

Stir well and let the sauce **simmer** very gently for a few minutes.

Then **strain** the sauce into a heated sauce boat and serve.

This sauce can always be prepared in advance and refrigerated.

RASPBERRY SAUCE

This utterly delicious accompaniment to a variety of fruits is more of a coulis than a sauce. A fruit coulis is nothing more than a liquid purée of fruit with a little sugar added, pressed and strained through a sieve.

Raspberries possess one of the most beautiful of all fruit tastes, and as they are soft already they do not need to be cooked before being easily liquefied into a coulis. Whether the result is technically a purée, a sauce or a coulis is of no importance. The result is delicious, and is enthusiastically recommended with baked peaches*.

Ingredients:
12 raspberries per person
a flat teaspoon of icing sugar per person

Sprinkle the fruit with as much icing sugar as you think appropriate for your taste – a flat teaspoonful per person will serve as a guide – **mix in** the sugar and **crush** the fruit with a wooden spoon and **press** it all through a sieve.

This will take a little time and effort, but the raspberries will eventually go through to produce an intense and juicy coulis.

---

* *Baked peaches, p.234*

PUDDINGS AND FRUIT DISHES

THE PUDDING AND FRUIT DISHES

The English word 'pudding' conjures up images of magnificent treacle, or ginger or lemon creations such as those traditionally made using butter, flour and eggs. And, dare I mention it, suet! Over the years the word 'pudding' has come to include any sweet course at the end of a meal whether a true pudding or not, and in any case no collection of sweet recipes which includes a traditional English Christmas pudding could possibly be entitled just Sweets or Desserts. However, most of the recipes are light and fruit based and so this chapter is therefore entitled 'The Pudding and Fruit Dishes'.

Many of the recipes have been inspired by French taste, and contain fruits which are prevalent in Provence. In Suffolk we are less fortunate, and so we have to be imaginative with long lasting fruits such as apples, pears, and quince, although we are saved by our strawberry season and our raspberries, the latter producing delicious fruits from summer until autumn when the late varieties provide a wonderful end to the growing year.

The fruit base of so many of the recipes is ideal from the perspective of healthy eating and also makes the dishes extremely easy to prepare. A watchful eye has been kept on sugar content and, where it has been possible to make reductions from the traditional levels the opportunity has been taken.

I have not ventured into pastry making. There are so many thousands of cooks throughout the length and breadth of the British Isles who are regular pastry makers that no instructions are needed from me, other than please always use natural butter rather than industrially produced margarine.

The recipe for the traditional Christmas pudding which I have included dates back in my family to the early Victorian era, but I should say that the one concession to modern thinking has been to replace the true suet ingredient with a vegetable based alternative. I am wondering whether I should have committed this English culinary crime. If I am aiding and abetting you to do the same, take no notice. Try the pudding with the real thing. Blow the suet, the fat and that awful moment on the bathroom scales when they register something which is, quite obviously. hopelessly inaccurate. It is Christmas after all.

APPLE COMPOTE WITH POMEGRANATE

This is the simplest possible recipe for using up surplus apples at the end of the season, or just because you like it at any time of year. The compote can be accompanied by almost anything you fancy, whether ice cream, yoghurt, Amaretti or shortbread. Anything made with almonds goes particularly well.

If you live in Suffolk you are bound to have plenty of Bramleys but, if not, come for the day in the Autumn. We are awash with apples then and they are practically given away.

Pomegranates are in season at about the same time as Bramleys are plentiful.

Ingredients (Serves 3)
1 kg of apples, (ideally Bramleys) after having been peeled and cored
1 dessertspoon of Demerara sugar
3 tablespoons of pomegranate seeds
4 tablespoons of water
1 small lemon, squeezed

Peel, core and cut up the apples. Pour the water into a lidded saucepan. Bring to the **boil** and immediately add the apples together with the sugar. **Stir**. **Add** the lemon juice and **stir** again. **Replace** the lid and **simmer** slowly.

If you are using Bramleys bear in mind that they cook extremely quickly and can turn into a mush in no time. Most other varieties will take around 25 minutes to become soft. When the compote has reached the consistency you like give it all a **stir** and let it cool. Make Demerara sugar available at the table especially if you have used the not very sweet Bramleys or another cooking variety.

When the compote is cool **sprinkle** the pomegranate seeds on each serving. Do not chill.

APPLE, PEAR AND WALNUT FLAN

This pudding is called a flan, primarily because there is no better name for it and if it had an open pastry case it would be a flan. Without the characteristic pastry case it makes a lighter end to any meal and is most enjoyable despite its simplicity.

A good bureaucrat would certainly call it APW, neatly avoiding the discussion, but its name is not important. It is a lovely, easy, autumnal dessert which combines the produce that many a country garden in England or France will yield.

Choose the variety of apples you prefer, and pears too, for all that has to be done is to cut up the fruit, crack the walnuts, put them all together and sprinkle with Demerara. And of course, warm it up a little.

Ingredients (Serves 4)
2 eating apples of choice, peeled and cored
2 pears of choice, peeled and cored
a very large handful of walnuts, cracked into halves
1 tablespoon of Demerara sugar
½ lemon, squeezed

Find an ovenproof flan dish in porcelain. **Core** the fruit and **slice** it, arranging it as attractively as you can around the dish. Try to emulate that wonderful French technique of arranging apple slices, overlapping one with another⋆.

Crack the walnuts carefully, obtaining as many unbroken halves as possible and place them on top of the fruit. **Sprinkle** with Demerara and lemon juice.

Under a medium grill **heat** the APW for about four minutes so as to melt the sugar and lightly warm the fruit. Then serve with yoghurt or ice cream.

⋆ *Preparing and arranging apple slices, p.231*

APRICOT COMPOTE

Although the idea of a compote does not always appeal given that so many fruits provide heavenly eating without being cooked at all, I always enjoy a compote of apricots so much that I would like to include it here, added to the advantage that to think of the South of France and apricots at the very same moment whisks you in a millisecond to the warmth of Provence.

The compote is wonderfully refreshing on its own so long as not too much sugar is added and the fresh tang of the apricots remains although it can be very simply complemented with a shortbread biscuit. Equally, it is delicious when served with Greek style yoghurt in the manner of the blackberry compote described later in this chapter.

Ingredients (Serves 4)
16 ripe apricots
2 tablespoons of Demerara sugar

Cover the apricots with water and heat them until the skins split. At that point **stir in** the Demerara and bring them to the boil. Let them **simmer** for two or three minutes. Then **drain** off the water. Spread the apricots out on a chopping board and **cut out** the stones. Cut up any large lumps of fruit.

Leave the apricots to cool.

AUTUMN PUDDING

Throughout this book there are recipes to be found which remind you of France – of sunshine – of long hot days – of Provence. This recipe, by contrast, is a potent reminder but of a different kind – of apples – of pears – of blackberries – of juicy Victoria plums gathered in a Suffolk orchard on days with autumn in the air. The sheer exhilaration of being in the countryside at this time of year, when the dry grasses crunch underfoot and where the hum of distant tractors tells of the freshly harvested stubble fields fast being turned from gold to brown is reflected in this gentle, sweet and so very comforting pudding which should be near the top of any cook's repertoire. Autumn pudding is easy to make and wonderful to eat and, like summer pudding, can readily be adjusted to the fruits available.

Ingredients (Serves 4)
1 large Bramley apple, peeled, cored and diced
4 fat Victoria plums, stoned and halved
170g blackberries
100g autumn raspberries
2 ripe pears, peeled cored and diced
1 orange, squeezed
2 tablespoons of sloe gin★
100–125g golden caster sugar
6–8 slices of white bread (avoid industrially produced white)

Prepare the fruits as above. **Plunge** the plums and blackberries into 250ml of boiling water for two minutes before adding the pears, apple and raspberries. Continue to boil for a further two to three minutes, **stirring** in the sugar till dissolved. Then **remove** from the heat and **add** the orange juice and sloe gin.

Line a pudding basin with slices of bread (remove the crusts) and fill with fruit reserving a little juice. **Cover** with bread and place a saucer on top to weigh the bread down. **Refrigerate**. Turn the pudding out carefully from the basin. Serve with Greek style yoghurt and the reserved juice if needed.

★ *Sloe gin, p.241*

WILD BLACKBERRY COMPOTE

It is a sad reflection that fewer people seem to be foraging along the hedgerows of Suffolk, or no doubt any other English county, than used to be so. That small group of mother and children moving along the hedges, dressed for a blustery Autumn day, little squeals of excitement being heard now and again as yet another wonderful flush of plump, ripe blackberries is found is a less frequent sight. The subtlety of taste of the wild blackberry is one of the most beguiling tastes of the countryside. Every moment spent blackberrying is a delight and part of a true country life.

Blackberry compote, served in alternate layers with Greek style yoghurt complements any meal, sophisticated or not.

Ingredients (Serves 4)
1 kg of wild blackberries
1 dessertspoon (or less) of castor sugar
250g of Greek style yoghurt

Cover the blackberries with water and gently bring them to the boil. As soon as they are soft **add** the sugar and stir it in well. **Strain**, and let the blackberries cool, breaking them up a little to make the compote.

An attractive way to serve the compote is to make alternate layers of the compote and the yoghurt in a tall glass. Use Greek style yoghurt, and, if available, the Suffolk-made yoghurt from Marybelle.

CHOCOLATE AND COFFEE VELVETS

Conventional chocolate mousse is so twentieth century, so dull! It is the kind of pudding you serve to satisfy everyone and offend no-one at a dinner of European finance ministers! In France it is very standard fare. At every small brasserie in France the waitress will turn into a automaton and sing out these words: *'Et comme dessert?'* You ask what she has, although you could repeat the answer in your sleep. *'Tarte aux pommes, crème caramel, mousse au chocolat, glace vanille'*. So I strongly recommend a variation upon the idea, not so rich, rather lighter and greatly more unusual. And to die for...!

Ingredients (Serves 4)
170g dark chocolate (preferably 85% cocoa solids) broken into squares
100g or less of white caster sugar
560ml (1pt) semi-skimmed milk
1 dessertspoon (not more) of freshly brewed strong coffee

Before you start, allow yourself at least 45 minutes to cook this dessert.. It is unfortunately rather a boring process as it needs constant stirring and attention.

Combine all the ingredients – although the coffee may be omitted if you prefer – in a heavy saucepan and bring to the **boil** carefully, **stirring** with a wooden spoon all the time. Watch that the contents do not boil over, and adjust the heat to achieve a very **gentle simmer**.

Stir for the next half an hour and listen to some soothing music, but **don't take your eyes off the saucepan**.

By this time the chocolate will have started to thicken, a process which will, as you stir, continue until the chocolate **covers the spoon thickly**. This is the critical point at which the chocolate should be poured into ramekins. Your judgement as to the suitable viscosity of the liquid is vital; it must not be too runny, yet not too thick.

Once poured allow it to set in the fridge for a couple of hours.

Note that the sweetness of this dessert is dependent on the balance between the sugar content of the chocolate you choose and the amount of sugar you add. My own preference is for less sugar and more oomph from the chocolate.

CHEESE AND FRUIT

An interminable argument never fades in Britain about cheese before pudding or pudding before cheese. It just won't go away! I know that any referendum would be won in Suffolk on pudding before cheese, but anywhere in France, with the possible exception of the English speaking Dordogne, the vote would be quite the opposite. It reminds me of the West Country battle as to whether the jam goes on the scone before the cream, to the horror of the Devonians and the approval of the Cornish, although as with the cheese referendum there would be pockets of resistance. A staunchly Devonian friend admits that the Cornish have got it right, as there is then no limit to the size of the dollop of cream!

Cheese and fruit is undoubtedly an agreeable and useful solution with which to finish a meal. Both Suffolk and Provence produce some wonderful cheeses, which give great pleasure. Cheese is of course very calorific, and higher in fats that many people feel they want or should have. It is worth bearing in mind that blue cheeses have a high fat content, whereas goats' cheese and some creamy cheeses from Northern France such as Coulommiers or Brie have less. Unfortunately, Roquefort and Stilton, which go so beautifully with ripe pears, have more or less the highest fat content of all. As a very rough rule of thumb one can reckon, generally speaking, that 25g of cheese will contain 100 calories.

A number of delicious cows' cheeses are made in Suffolk, amongst them Suffolk Gold and Suffolk Blue. If you are near Bungay you will find the truly outstanding Baron Bigod, a traditional raw milk creamy white cheese with a bloomy rind in the manner of French Brie de Meaux. It is made from the milk of a herd of Monbeliarde cows which were specially brought to Suffolk from the French Alps, and is named after the Earl who was responsible for building Bungay Castle in the C12.

In Provence, local ewes' and goats' milk cheeses are abundant and sit side by side with wonderful fruits in every town and village market. Well known is the nutty flavoured Banon, a cheese which can be made from cows', goats' or ewes' milk and is steeped in brandy. It is at its best during the Summer months. It is easily recognisable being wrapped in chestnut leaves tied with raffia. Then there are the Brousses, made during the colder months from goats' or ewes' milk. These mild cheeses are white and creamy and often served with cooked or fresh fruits.

Berries, cherries, pears and apples marry beautifully with many cheeses from both France and England. Together they can make a wonderful dessert and can often give more pleasure than creations which have taken hours to make from complicated recipes. Cheese with fruit is an excellent combination not to be ignored.

CHRISTMAS PUDDING

This pudding I have known since childhood. It is a true recipe from early Victorian England used by my great great grandmother and my mother's family since that time. I can certainly vouch for the wonders of this pudding, from long experience.

I remember the recipe being used Christmas after Christmas. It was always an important ritual to stir it endlessly which one does not forget how to do! Stirring is quite vital so please do not skimp on it. A large porcelain bowl and a huge wooden spoon is needed, or at least the spoon always seemed huge to a small boy, but something pretty sturdy is essential.

Ingredients (English Imperial measures)

½ lb large stoned raisins	1oz chopped almonds	¼ teaspoon salt
¼ lb currants	3ozs flour	1/8 pint of pale ale
¼ lb sultanas	3ozs breadcrumbs	(traditionally Worthingtons
¼ lb shredded suet	3oz apple, grated	which was popular in
(or vegetable alternative)	rind of 1 orange, grated	Victorian times)
¼ lb Demerara sugar	rind of 1 lemon, grated	2 large eggs
2ozs mixed peel	1 teaspoon mixed spice	½ wineglass of cognac

Mix the dry ingredients. **Add** the liquids and mix well. **Stir** and **stir** as much as possible. Leave overnight.

Stir again, and put the mixture into a large buttered basin. Cover the top of the basin with greaseproof paper and tie it securely with string. Then envelop the basin in a piece of muslin and tie it at the top.

Put the basin in a steamer or a large lidded saucepan of boiling water and **steam** for 6 to 8 hours.(If you have a steamer the process is much easier with no risk of water getting into the pudding). **Make sure** the water is kept topped up. **It is vital** that the pudding does not dry out while cooking.

Keep the pudding tied up in the paper and muslin and **steam it again** for 3 to 4 hours on the day it is to be eaten.

This quantity will make one large pudding, providing around 10 portions. The tradition is to make a smaller one at the same time and store it in a cool place until Easter. It will last until the following Christmas if so wished.

FRUIT GRATIN

There are few puddings more comforting than a traditional English fruit crumble with a thick, crunchy layer of crumble to make one feel replete or, sometimes, rather more replete than is comfortable. This recipe is the French take on the idea, and especially delicious it is too. It gives a much lighter touch than any pastry or traditional English crumble can bring. The recipe can be used successfully with whatever fruits are in season. It is wonderful with raspberries alone, raspberries and strawberries mixed, strawberries alone, blackberry and apple, or with raspberries and rhubarb.

Use a round ovenproof open flan dish. Because the appeal of this pudding is its lightness, a larger dish will need the total weight of the topping to be proportionate to the area of the dish so that the lightness of character is not altered. This does, though, require a calculation using πr^2.

> **Ingredients for a 20cm open flan dish (Serves 3–4)**
> 50g of cold butter
> 50g of Demerara sugar (or caster)
> 50g of Woodbridge Tide Mill flour if available, or plain white flour
> fruit to cover the base of the dish

Preheat the oven to Gas 5, 190C.

Mix the flour with the sugar using a blender. Then take the butter **from the fridge, dice it** and add it to the mixed flour and sugar. Then **blend** all three ingredients together so that the mixture has the consistency of breadcrumbs. This takes only a few seconds. **If the butter is at room temperature the operation will not work.**

Cover the whole area of the flan dish with the fruit, but **do not heap it up**. Each piece of fruit should lie directly on the base of the dish. **Sprinkle the flour/sugar/butter mixture evenly all over the fruit. It will not cover it perfectly. Bake** for 30 minutes.

Note: If slicing apples or pears, cut them in half down the stalk, core them, place the halves flat side down on a chopping board and slice them very thinly. These slices will look attractive if they just overlap each other on the open flan dish.

ORANGES IN A HONEY AND ROSEMARY SAUCE

So often one seems stuck to think of an attractive dessert. It needs to be simple, quick to make and not swimming in sugars and fats, and also one that retains the balance of the meal. A good dinner can so easily be ruined by too heavy an ending, no matter how delicious that ending may be. I think about this problem every time I see sticky toffee pudding on a restaurant menu, which it invariably is when you have eaten too much already. Orange slices drenched in a sauce made from lightweight honey and rosemary is often an excellent answer, but ensure the oranges are juicy, not pithy, and in season.

Ingredients (Serves 4)
2 large and juicy oranges
150ml of water
2 teaspoons of honey
2 good sized sprigs of fresh rosemary

Slice the oranges **thinly**, and **cut off** the peel and **remove** the pith. **Save** the juice released by the cutting. Place the slices on a flat plate such as a large flan dish. Remove any pips.

Combine the honey and water in a saucepan, and add the sprigs of rosemary. Slowly bring the pan to the boil and **simmer** for about 10 minutes, by which time the sauce should be beginning to **reduce** slightly.

Remove the rosemary and pour the sauce over the oranges.

Leave it all to cool and place it in the fridge until required.

PEACHES WITH A RASPBERRY PURÉE

This looks most sophisticated when nicely presented, yet it is simplicity itself to prepare. It is somewhat reminiscent of Escoffier's famous Pêches Cardinal but without the Kirsch, ice cream and almonds. It does not take a great deal of effort, should your imagination be sufficiently stimulated, to emulate the great man himself! However, this is a simplified version which is nevertheless extremely delicious. It will transport you back to C19 Paris even if it is not the real thing! It will give much pleasure.

Ingredients (for each person)
1 peach per person, fully ripe and ready to eat
12 raspberries per person for the purée; plus
5 raspberries per person for each portion
1 teaspoon of icing sugar

Prepare a cold raspberry purée by sprinkling raspberries with a teaspoon of icing sugar, or more if they are a little sharp, and **pressing** them through a **fine** sieve with a wooden spoon. This will take a little time and effort, but the raspberries will eventually go through to produce a juicy purée. Set the purée on one side, ready to pour over the peaches.

Then **immerse** the peaches for 30 to 40 seconds in a saucepan of vigorously boiling water. **Remove them** from the water promptly, **halve** them and extract the stone. The skin will come away cleanly when pinched between two fingers.

Place them on the plates upon which they will be served, and **pour** the purée over them. **Add** five fresh raspberries to each serving.

BAKED PEACHES (OR NECTARINES) WITH REDCURRANTS

Outside Suffolk few people have heard of a 'crinkle-crankle' wall. Unlike our medieval moats of which there are several hundred in the county adorning the landscape around great houses, manors and important farms, crinkle-crankles are few and far between. The kitchen gardens of a number of great houses benefited from crinkle-crankles which were used to force plants by offering both sunlight and shelter, especially to exotic fruits, but these days our peaches are necessarily imported. However, make sure the quality of the fruit is good and the individual fruits are properly ripe. A sprig of fresh redcurrants will add style, colour and taste.

Ingredients (Serves 4)
4 peaches or nectarines, peeled
1 orange, freshly squeezed
2 heaped teaspoons of icing sugar
a good sprig of fresh redcurrants

Preheat the oven to Gas 7, 220C.

Choose the best ripe fruits that you can find.

Immerse the peaches for 25 to 30 seconds in a saucepan of vigorously boiling water. **Remove them** from the water promptly, **halve** them and extract the stone. The skin will come away cleanly when pinched between two fingers.

Place them flat side down on a baking tray. **Squeeze** an orange and pour the juice over them. Then **sprinkle** them with icing sugar.

Bake for 15 minutes. Serve with all the juices from the baking tray. **Garnish** with the sprig of redcurrants.

Redcurrants

POACHED PEARS

There is no fruit more characteristic of Suffolk than the pear. Anyone who has lived in the county for a long time will, when pears are mentioned, immediately imagine one of those old Suffolk orchards – huge pear trees, moon high, unpruned, uncultivated, unkempt. The inevitable goose will be honking quietly away at the foot of a tree in the hope that yet another over-ripe fruit will come its way. The peace and sunshine which permeate that ancient place, encompassed by tall ash and bushy hawthorn, will remain undisturbed for hours on end as the fruit silently ripens.

Perfect ripeness is, of course, the pre-requisite for satisfactory culinary use, but ripeness is a state that arrives imperceptibly, silently and often so quickly that the cook has to be quick to catch that magic moment to get the very best from the crop.

Ingredients (Serves 4)
4 pears at the point of ripeness, peeled, cored but with stalk remaining
red wine to cover (at Christmas try mulled wine)
1 vanilla bean, split
a pinch of ground cinnamon
1 teaspoon of Demerara sugar

Peel and core the pears whole. Leave the stalk in place.

Place them in a saucepan and **cover** them with red wine and **add** a vanilla bean **split** lengthways. **Add** the sugar and **heat** gently. Within a short time the pears will begin to soften. This will be the best moment to **add** the pinch of cinnamon. Now simmer them very gently for 20 minutes before removing them from the heat and **allowing** them to cool. **Save** the liquid for sauce.

To make the sauce simply **reduce** the poaching liquid. Keep it warm and serve it over the cooled pears with a little yoghurt, vanilla ice cream or pouring cream.

PRUNES IN RED WINE

Prunes have an unjustifiably poor reputation in Britain, largely because they are considered to be nothing more than a rather convenient breakfast food with particular remedial uses. Oh dear! How could we get it so wrong?

This dessert will change any such preconceptions for ever and you will be clamouring for the very best prunes *(pruneaux)* which come from Ente plums *(prunes)* grown in the Agen district in South West France.

Ingredients (Serves 4)
250g prunes, carefully pitted
250ml of good red wine from South West France, ideally Buzet
250ml of water
3 tablespoons of caster sugar
a long strip of orange zest
a long strip of lemon zest
1 vanilla pod, split and scraped

Combine all the ingredients apart from the prunes and heat them gently until boiling point is reached. Then **simmer** them quietly for a few minutes. The liquid will thicken a little as it simmers.

Once it has thickened a little **add** the prunes and **gently simmer** the whole for about 20 minutes. By this time the prunes will be thoroughly cooked, and the ensemble can be put in a large bowl to cool.

Let it all rest without being disturbed for at least a couple of hours – 24 hours if you wish. It just gets better and better as the different flavours meld together.

Strain, and **serve** at room temperature.

SUGARED CLEMENTINES

Oh what magic this simple little dish will bring! The easiest ever, the quickest to prepare ever and one of the most delicious of all fruit desserts.

Clementines are a hybrid of the Seville orange and the tangerine and are primarily grown around the Mediterranean. Their only disadvantage is that when the winter season comes to an end in February we have to wait until October for more.

This is a stunner. I cannot stop making it when the fruits are good.

Ingredients (Serves 4)
6 or 8 juicy, seedless clementines
icing sugar

Peel the clementines carefully, and **remove** any remaining pithy pieces.

Gently pull each fruit apart into two equal portions.

Place each half, flat side down, in a bowl large enough to accommodate them all comfortably.

Find a sharp fork – those old fish forks seem to have prongs as sharp as pins – and **prick** each half several times so that their juice starts to seep.

Now **sprinkle** half a teaspoonful of icing sugar, or more if you wish, on top of each half, and **refrigerate**. The seeping juices will be soaked up by the icing sugar.

Leave undisturbed for at least two hours before serving. By this time more juice will have seeped out into the icing sugar to making a hard, sugary crust. Heaven!

Serve straight from the fridge.

ROASTED STRAWBERRIES

This is an impressive finale to a good meal. It is light, refreshing and the flavour is intense. It can be served alone, or if an accompaniment is wanted a roast peach makes an excellent partner. It is extremely easy to make. The strawberries do not have to be perfect.

Ingredients (Serves 2)
25 strawberries
1 dessertspoon of castor sugar
1 dessertspoon of balsamic vinegar
a few green peppercorns, whole

Preheat the oven to Gas 6, 200C.

Slice the strawberries in half. **Spread** them out in a small ovenproof dish preferably of porcelain and **add** the balsamic vinegar and the green peppercorns. **Stir** them around, then **sprinkle** the sugar over them and **stir** again.

Leave for a good 10 minutes before roasting.

Roast in the ovenproof dish for 10 minutes. **Serve hot**, perhaps with a scoop of vanilla ice cream, or fat free yoghurt if preferred.

VANILLA APRICOTS

An easy, relatively unusual and attractive dessert may be made simply from fresh apricots and vanilla sugar.

To make vanilla sugar take two vanilla pods and put them in a lidded jam jar full of caster sugar. Keep the vanilla and sugar together permanently; this will allow the vanilla pods to impart a delicate flavour to the sugar – shake it up from time to time – which can be used for a variety of purposes.

Ingredients (Serves 4)
12 or 16 fresh apricots
vanilla sugar
water

Preheat the oven to Gas 1, 140C.

Place the apricots in a flat bottomed oven-proof dish. **Remove** any stalk which may be left and stand each fruit upright.

Pour a teaspoonful of vanilla sugar on top of each apricot.

Pour a small amount of cold water into the dish, sufficient to cover the bottom, and so that the apricots are sitting in a shallow pool of water.

Place the dish carefully – the apricots have a tendency to fall over easily – in a cool oven for about 40 minutes.

SLOE GIN

Sloe gin, or the very similar and (dare I say it) slightly superior damson gin, is one of those traditions that none of us who lives in the country want to be without. The disadvantage of sloe gin is is that it is exceedingly strong, and the occasions which arise in modern life when one feels one would like to have a swig (but perhaps that is not the right word) seem to be relatively few. It was all rather different fifty years ago but we now live in the C21.

One cannot think of going shooting without it (in England, of course) as it undoubtedly improves one's aim, or if not one's aim the bag one thinks one has brought in... but not everyone shoots! In France, a champagne lunch at the start of a shoot for wild boar runs it pretty close for side effects.

Sloe gin is undoubtedly a wonderful drink, but I do think it has a culinary use which outweighs the traditions of the English shooting field. It is extraordinarily good when added to a traditional English trifle, and even better when added to an Autumn Pudding★ for which there is a recipe in this book.

The principal requirement is a nicely fruiting blackthorn bush, which should be covered with sloes in the autumn. I am lucky enough to have a beautiful blackthorn bush, and in case it does not fruit particularly well in any year there are always the damson trees...

Ingredients
Sufficient sloes to half fill an empty gin bottle
Demerara sugar, 1gm per 10ml
a bottle of organic gin

Prick every sloe twice so that they slowly bleed. **Half fill** the empty gin bottle with the sloes, **add** the sugar (75g for a standard bottle), and **top up** the bottle with gin. **Cork** the bottle and **leave** for at least 6 weeks, turning occasionally. If made in early November it will be ready to decant by Christmas.

★ *Autumn pudding, p.226*

Spring produce

EPILOGUE

The contrasts and similarities found by comparing an English county having ambitions to become the most admired food destination in Britain and a dramatically dissimilar region in the South of France, known throughout the world for its own lifestyle, landscape, culture, climate and cuisine, are remarkable. However, when one stops a while for quiet reflection and sits in the sun on a convenient milestone one comes to realise there is a very happy relationship between the two.

I ask you to imagine that, at the conclusion of this journey, we are now all sitting together on the terrace in the dappled sunshine at Les Deux Garçons, that famous brasserie once frequented by Cezanne and his friend Emile Zola on the Cours Mirabeau in Aix-en-Provence. I hope we would all agree, perhaps over a cool glass of Côtes-de-Provence, that every step in our journey together had been worthwhile and that the very idea of reading a recipe or the prospect of learning to cook were not the horrors we once thought them to be.

APPENDIX
KITCHEN JARGON

The following terms are not necessarily obvious, and some rather curious.

Al dente means vegetables which are crisp to the bite and hardly cooked through.

Baking means to cook in an open baking dish in the oven so as to preserve and assimilate the flavours of the foods in the dish. This contrasts with roasting which usually means cooking in the oven at a high temperature. My own rule of thumb is that 200C is the point at which baking becomes roasting, although the distinction does not seem to matter very much.

Baste means to spoon hot cooking liquids (such as those produced from roasting meat) on to the item being roasted to prevent it from drying up.

Blanching means to immerse in boiling water for a very short time.

Blending has a particular meaning in this book – it is used to indicate that you need to use the electric hand held blender to produce a smooth mixture such as a soup or a purée.

Braising means to cook food very slowly for a long time in a liquid that is hardly simmering. It is often used for cuts of meat that need to become tender or certain vegetables such as cabbage or onion.

Browning means to heat meat or poultry, often by frying gently, in order to seal in the juices or in the case of minced beef or other meats to let the surplus fat run off. It does not necessarily mean to turn things truly brown, rather to take away the rawness and give them a lightly cooked colour.

Clarified butter means butter which has been melted, the sediment left aside and the scum removed. It is used mainly for emulsified sauces, that is to say sauces made from two immiscible liquids.

Cleaning and gutting a fish means the process of removing its internal organs and washing it ready for cooking.

Coating means to cover evenly like a thick coat of paint.

De-glazing means that the cooking juices and sediments left in a pan (for example after roasting meat) are heated together with wine or stock to make a sauce, preferably after the excess fats have been skimmed off.

Dicing means to cut into cubes, sometimes as large as two or three centimetres square, or as small as you can possibly cut by hand or with a gadget.

Dry-frying is to fry without the addition of any cooking oils to the pan. It is used for very fatty foods such as chorizo sausage.

Filleting a fish means to remove the bone structure of a raw fish leaving the flesh ready for cooking.

Folding-in means to mix foods – an example is mixing molten chocolate with egg white – very gently and in a churning motion so that the air is not removed by rapid and insensitive movements which would ruin the structure of the mixture. Folding is rather an odd word for this activity

Lardons are small chunks of pork fat (often from a pork belly) or bacon added to the cooking, for example in a stew.

Marinate is to use a liquid called a marinade made from wine, herbs, olive oil, garlic, and similar aromatics in which meat is soaked prior to cooking. To make a dry marinade coat a joint with olive oil and rub in dried herbs.

Parboiling means to boil foods for a short while so that they become only partially cooked.

Reducing means to reduce the volume of a liquid by evaporation through heating in order to intensify flavours and aromas, e.g. wine is often reduced for sauce.

Roux is a mixture of butter and flour cooked together as a base for a sauce.

Searing means to place meat or fish in a very hot pan for a very short time so that the outside of the meat or fish is rapidly cooked, thus sealing in its juices and leaving the interior virtually uncooked.

Seasoning means to add salt and pepper, or possibly some herbal flavouring if specifically instructed.

Scaling a fish means to remove the scales, usually with a wire brush, prior to cooking.

Simmering means to retain a liquid very close to boiling point but so that it shudders and shakes but hardly bubbles.

Stir frying means to fry in an oiled pan at a high heat very quickly. The Chinese do this in a wok.

Stock is a cooking liquid made from meat, poultry, fish or vegetables. Stock is added to a dish to provide additional moisture while cooking. Stock is the base liquid of most soups. It can be made from stock cubes (always use organic cubes) which are widely sold or from boiling meat or fish bones (preferably turbot bones) which professional chefs would have time to do.

Vanilla sugar is white caster sugar which has been flavoured with vanilla by putting vanilla beans into the sugar during storage.

TEN PERSONAL FAVOURITES

Tomato tapenade *(page 30)*
This is a traditional Provençal condiment – intense, powerful and delicious yet extremely simple to make.

Watercress and tomato soup with poached egg *(page 48)*
This is one of the very best of all the vegetable soups.

Cod cheeks in a Provençal style *(page 89)*
Cheeky this recipe most certainly is, as I have matched the fish with a Provençal style sauce most presumptuously.

Sea trout poached whole *(page 125)*
A poached wild sea trout is really the high point of this book. Yet it is one of the easiest recipes to achieve.

Daube aux pruneaux *(page 137)*
This is a sensationally satisfying and warming stew, and although long, slow cooking is needed it can be put together in minutes.

Diced shoulder of mutton stewed in real ale *(page 145)*
This is a particularly delicious, very English, recipe.

Roast Suffolk chicken breasts with Suffolk plums *(page 159)*
Suffolk is very well known for both its poultry and its wonderful plums.

Chicken sauté à la Provençale *(page 162)*
Like so much cooking which originates from the South of France, it leaves you satisfied yet with a sense of contentment and well-being rather than a legacy of over-indulgence.

Roast loin of wild venison *(page 176)*
We are lucky in East Suffolk to have venison from Rendlesham forest or Dunwich at hand, although there are many other places in the British Isles and in France where superb wild venison can be found.

Mixed game stew *(page 178)*
I have developed this recipe over many successive stews, and the lengthy list of ingredients should not discourage you. The results are really worthwhile.

ACKNOWLEDGEMENTS

Most cookery books will have a section acknowledging the helpfulness of all those people who have provided recipes or participated in its production. This book is entirely different in concept. It is a personal story, pure and simple, but a story I want to share, because I hope it will persuade many others to follow in my footsteps which have given me a great deal of interest and happiness.

There are a number of people without whom I could not have learnt to cook and others who have been instrumental in making the book it is.

First and foremost is my wife Karen who has given her unfailing support to the project for several years, has painted a lovely watercolour of a woodcock, and has loyally eaten recipe after recipe practically every day of her life for a very long time and considered with me change after change so as to ensure that the best possible result ensued. To her I am eternally grateful.

Particular and very special thanks go to the distinguished artist Tessa Newcomb for her wonderful paintings which make the book what it is, and for her deep understanding of Suffolk and its food and produce so brilliantly portrayed. My thanks also go to Jason Gathorne-Hardy for his delightful drawings of farm animals for which he is so well known.

I would like to give very special thanks to Lisbeth Jensen for so kindly proofreading the manuscript most diligently, and for all her helpful suggestions. Another person who has supported the project with great enthusiasm and skill is Deborah Mack, formerly Manager of Potterton Books in London. Her advice and flair from both an artistic and commercial viewpoint has been greatly appreciated.

Many people have been most generous in conversation, and between them I have learnt a great deal, especially Chris Wightman of Maximus Sustainable Fishing at Friday Street near Aldeburgh whose fascinating shop and excellent fish never fail to please. I would also like to thank Jason of Mains Restaurant in Yoxford, Michael, Paul and Dan, butchers at Creaseys of Peasenhall, Ian the butcher at Friday Street Butchery, Agnès Clough of Framlingham for checking Fish in French, Peter Harrison, the Suffolk chef, for his most delicious recipe and to various friends and family members who have tried many of my suggestions. Grateful thanks also go to Douglas Atfield for his superb photography of the artwork presented on these pages.

My thanks go to the team at Lavenham Press for their patient advice and help, especially Alex Ford who designed the book and who has been a great pleasure to work with.

Finally, I am most grateful to Lady Cranbrook, President of The Aldeburgh Food & Drink Festival for her interest in the project and for so kindly writing the Foreword. She is the greatest possible ambassadress for Suffolk and its food and I am honoured to include her Foreword in the book.

INDEX